Preface

1. Introduction   **6**

1.1 A Brief History of APIs   *7*

1.2 Why Choose RESTful APIs?   *11*

1.3 Introduction to Node.js   *15*

1.4 Tools and Setup   *19*

2. Understanding REST   **23**

2.1 Introduction to REST   *24*

2.2 REST Principles   *28*

2.3 HTTP Methods for RESTful Services   *34*

2.4 Designing RESTful APIs   *38*

3. Setting Up Your Environment   **43**

3.1 Installing Node.js and NPM   *44*

3.2 Setting Up a Project Directory   *47*

3.3 Configuring Environment Variables   *50*

3.4 Installing Essential Packages   *54*

4. Introduction to Node.js   **58**

4.1 What is Node.js?   *59*

4.2 Setting Up Node.js   *63*

4.3 Node.js Architecture   *67*

4.4 Basic Node.js Modules   *72*

5. Building a Basic Server   **77**

5.1 Setting Up Your Development Environment   *78*

5.2 Writing Your First Node.js Server   *82*

5.3 Configuring Routes   *86*

5.4 Handling Requests and Responses   *90*

6. Working with Express.js   **95**

6.1. Introduction to Express.js   *96*

6.2. Setting Up Express.js   *100*

6.3. Building Basic Routes   *104*

6.4. Middleware Functions and Usage   *107*

7. Middleware Functions   **111**

7.1 Introduction to Middleware Functions   *112*

7.2 Creating Custom Middleware   *116*

7.3 Using Third-party Middleware   *120*

7.4 Error Handling Middleware Functions   *127*

8. Routing in Express   **133**

8.1 Routing Basics   *134*

8.2 Route Parameters   *138*

8.3 Handling Different HTTP Methods   *142*

8.4 Middleware in Routes   *146*

9. Connecting to a Database   **151**

9.1 Choosing a Database   *152*

9.2 Setting Up the Database   *156*

9.3 Connecting Node.js to the Database   *160*

9.4 Handling Database Connections and Errors   *165*

10. Handling Authentication and Authorization   **170**

10.1 Introduction to Authentication and Authorization   *171*

10.2 Implementing JSON Web Tokens (JWT)   *175*

10.3 Securing Endpoints with Middleware   *181*

10.4 Role-Based Access Control (RBAC)   *185*

11. Testing and Debugging   **190**

11.1 Unit Testing   *191*

11.2 Integration Testing   *196*

11.3 Debugging Techniques   *201*

11.4 Mocking and Stubbing   *206*

12. Glossary   **211**

Glossary   **212**

Preface

Welcome to "Building RESTful APIs with Node.js".

In an era where data and connectivity drive the world forward, understanding and implementing RESTful APIs is an invaluable skill for any developer. This book aims to be your companion on a journey through the world of RESTful API development using Node.js, bringing together fundamental concepts, practical examples, and the latest best practices.

This book was generated by artificial intelligence to provide a systematic and consistent approach to building RESTful APIs. Our goal is to offer insightful guidance for both beginners and experienced developers who wish to broaden their understanding of how to create APIs in an efficient, scalable, and secure manner.

Why this book? The landscape of API development is constantly evolving. Node.js, with its event-driven, non-blocking I/O, offers a lightweight and efficient way to build fast and scalable network applications. Combining Node.js with REST principles enables developers to create robust and maintainable APIs that can seamlessly handle a multitude of client requests. This book is designed to be a practical guide, breaking down complex concepts into easy-to-follow steps.

The journey presented in this book starts with the basics of REST and Node.js, then gradually builds up to advanced topics like authentication, authorization, and testing. The following chapters have been meticulously organized to enhance your learning experience:

1. **Introduction**
2. **Understanding REST**
3. **Setting Up Your Environment**
4. **Introduction to Node.js**
5. **Building a Basic Server**

6. **Working with Express.js**
7. **Middleware Functions**
8. **Routing in Express**
9. **Connecting to a Database**
10. **Handling Authentication and Authorization**
11. **Testing and Debugging**
12. **Glossary**

By the end of this book, you will have a comprehensive understanding of how to build, deploy, and manage RESTful APIs with Node.js, harnessing the power and flexibility offered by this powerful runtime environment.

Let's embark on this exciting journey together. Happy coding!

1. Introduction

1.1 A Brief History of APIs

The concept of an Application Programming Interface (API) has evolved significantly throughout the history of computing. From its origins in the early days of programming to its current role in creating interconnected web services, APIs have continually shaped how developers build applications. This subchapter explores the key milestones in the history of APIs, providing context for their evolution and their pivotal role in modern software development.

Early Days of APIs

APIs date back to the 1960s when the concept of subroutines or function calls was introduced in programming. These early APIs allowed different parts of a program to interact with each other, making code more modular and reusable. A simple example of early API usage can be captured in the concept of library functions such as printf in C:

```c
#include <stdio.h>

int main() {
    printf("Hello, World!\n");
    return 0;
}
```

This function call to printf can be considered an early example of an API, where printf is part of a library that provides predefined functionality.

The Rise of Web APIs

The internet's growth in the 1990s brought a significant leap forward in the use of APIs. Web APIs allowed different web services to interact, enabling more complex and integrated systems. These APIs typically used protocols like HTTP to facilitate communication between client and server.

In the early days of web APIs, SOAP (Simple Object Access Protocol) was a popular protocol for exchanging structured information. SOAP APIs used XML-based messaging, which was both verbose and rigid, yet it provided a standard way to interact with web services.

An example of a SOAP request might look like this:

```
<?xml version="1.0"?>
<soap:Envelope xmlns:soap="http://schemas.xmlsoap.org/soap/
envelope/">
    <soap:Body>
        <GetTemperature>
            <City>New York</City>
        </GetTemperature>
    </soap:Body>
</soap:Envelope>
```

The Emergence of REST

Despite SOAP's popularity, developers sought simpler, more flexible methods for web service interaction. This demand gave rise to Representational State Transfer (REST), a more lightweight and easier-to-use alternative. RESTful APIs use standard HTTP methods like GET, POST, PUT, and DELETE, and typically exchange data in formats like JSON or XML.

A RESTful API request is much more straightforward compared to SOAP, as seen in the following example:

```
GET http://api.weather.com/temperature?city=New+York
```

The server response might return JSON data:

```
{
    "city": "New York",
    "temperature": "20°C"
}
```

REST in the Era of Node.js

Node.js, introduced in 2009, revolutionized server-side programming by enabling JavaScript to run on the server. This shift allowed developers to use a single programming language for both client and server-side code. Node.js, with its non-blocking I/O and event-driven architecture, became an excellent choice for building scalable and performant RESTful APIs.

A basic example of a RESTful API in Node.js with Express.js might look like this:

```
const express = require('express');
const app = express();

app.get('/temperature', (req, res) => {
    const city = req.query.city;
    // For the sake of example, we return a static temperat
ure
    res.json({ city: city, temperature: '20°C' });
});

app.listen(3000, () => {
    console.log('Server is running on http://localhost:3000
');
});
```

This simple API listens for GET requests on the /temperature endpoint, retrieves the city query parameter, and returns a JSON response.

The Future of APIs

APIs continue to evolve with the advancement of technologies like GraphQL, which offers more flexibility and efficiency compared to REST. GraphQL allows clients to request exactly the data they need, reducing payload size and improving application performance.

Although the focus of this book is on building RESTful APIs with Node.js, it is essential to recognize the fluidity and continuous development within the API landscape. As technologies and requirements evolve, API paradigms will further adapt to meet the changing needs of software development.

Understanding the history of APIs provides valuable context as we embark on building RESTful APIs with Node.js. With a solid grasp of the past, we can better appreciate the tools and techniques available today and anticipate future developments in the API domain.

1.2 Why Choose RESTful APIs?

When building modern web applications, the choice of API architecture can have a significant impact on the development experience, scalability, and maintainability of your application. RESTful APIs (Representational State Transfer) have emerged as a popular choice for API design, providing a robust, straightforward approach to creating networked applications. Here are some compelling reasons to choose RESTful APIs:

Simplicity and Ease of Use

One of the primary reasons developers lean towards RESTful APIs is their simplicity. REST is based on standard HTTP methods, such as GET, POST, PUT, and DELETE, which are easy to understand and implement. This method relies on well-defined conventions, making it easier for developers to create and consume APIs without the need for extensive documentation or complex protocols.

```
GET /api/users
POST /api/users
PUT /api/users/{id}
DELETE /api/users/{id}
```

Statlessness

RESTful APIs are stateless, meaning each request from a client to the server must contain all the information needed to understand and process the request. This stateless nature simplifies the server design and increases scalability since the server does not need to store any session-related information.

```
GET /api/orders/{order_id} HTTP/1.1
Host: www.example.com
Authorization: Bearer some_access_token
```

Scalability

By adhering to a stateless protocol, RESTful APIs ensure that each request is independent of others, which significantly aids in scaling horizontally. Load balancers can distribute incoming requests to multiple servers, and servers can be added or removed without disrupting the interactions between the client and the server.

Flexibility and Evolvability

RESTful APIs are designed to be flexible, allowing various representations of resources, such as JSON, XML, or even plain text. This flexibility means clients can choose the most appropriate format for their needs, making it easier to evolve and extend the API over time without breaking existing clients.

```
{
  "user_id": 1,
  "name": "John Doe",
  "email": "john.doe@example.com"
}
```

Cacheability

HTTP has built-in support for caching, which can be leveraged by RESTful APIs to enhance performance. By properly using HTTP headers such as Cache-Control, ETag, and Expires, response data can be cached, reducing the need for repeated database queries and decreasing server load.

```
GET /api/products HTTP/1.1
Host: www.example.com
Cache-Control: max-age=3600
```

Uniform Interface

The uniform interface is a key constraint of RESTful architecture. It defines a standard way of crafting resources and their interactions using URIs, HTTP methods, media types, and hypermedia. This uniformity simplifies API consumption, as developers can predict the API behavior without needing to understand the specific logic of each endpoint.

```
GET /api/articles
Accept: application/json
```

Wide Adoption and Tooling

RESTful APIs are widely adopted across various industries and platforms, resulting in a robust ecosystem of tools and libraries for testing, monitoring, and documentation. Tools like Postman for testing, Swagger for documentation, and various Node.js libraries make it easier to develop and maintain RESTful APIs.

```json
{
  "openapi": "3.0.0",
  "info": {
    "title": "Sample API",
    "version": "1.0.0"
  },
  "paths": {
    "/api/users": {
      "get": {
        "summary": "Get all users",
        "responses": {
          "200": {
            "description": "A list of users."
          }
        }
      }
    }
  }
}
```

Strong Fidelity with HTTP

RESTful APIs align closely with the HTTP protocol, utilizing its features, status codes, and methods. This high fidelity with HTTP allows for a more intuitive interaction model and leverages existing web infrastructure and standards.

```
POST /api/login HTTP/1.1
Host: www.example.com
Content-Type: application/json

{
  "username": "john_doe",
  "password": "password123"
}
```

Conclusion

Choosing RESTful APIs for your Node.js applications provides a well-understood, scalable, and flexible approach to designing networked systems. The simplicity of using standard HTTP methods, allied with a rich ecosystem of supportive tools and libraries, makes RESTful APIs an excellent choice for modern web development. Their statelessness, cacheability, and strong fidelity with HTTP further enhance their robustness and performance, making them an industry-standard for API development.

1.3 Introduction to Node.js

Node.js is a powerful, event-driven, non-blocking I/O runtime environment that allows developers to build scalable and high-performance web applications with ease. Built on the V8 JavaScript engine, Node.js enables the execution of JavaScript code on the server side, making it an essential tool for modern web development.

What is Node.js?

Node.js is an open-source, cross-platform runtime environment specifically designed for server-side and networking applications. Its asynchronous and event-driven architecture allows it to handle multiple connections concurrently, making it an ideal choice for building RESTful APIs. Node.js was created by Ryan Dahl in 2009 and has since gained immense popularity among developers due to its efficiency and scalability.

Key Features of Node.js

Asynchronous and Non-blocking I/O

One of the core features of Node.js is its asynchronous and non-blocking I/O operations. This means that Node.js can handle multiple I/O operations simultaneously without waiting for any operation to complete. It uses a single-threaded event loop to process all asynchronous callbacks.

```
const fs = require('fs');

fs.readFile('/path/to/file', 'utf-8', (err, data) => {
  if (err) {
    console.error(err);
  } else {
    console.log(data);
  }
});
console.log('This will print first');
```

In the above code snippet, `fs.readFile` reads the file asynchronously, allowing the code to continue execution without waiting for the file read operation to complete.

Event-Driven Architecture

Node.js follows an event-driven architecture, meaning it uses events to handle asynchronous operations. This allows Node.js to manage a large number of concurrent connections efficiently.

```
const http = require('http');

const server = http.createServer((req, res) => {
  res.statusCode = 200;
  res.setHeader('Content-Type', 'text/plain');
  res.end('Hello, World!\n');
});

server.on('connection', () => {
  console.log('A new connection was made.');
});

server.listen(3000, '127.0.0.1', () => {
  console.log('Server running at http://127.0.0.1:3000/');
});
```

Here, the `http.createServer` method creates a server that listens for requests and emits events such as `connection`.

Single-Threaded but Highly Scalable

Node.js uses a single-threaded model with event looping, making it highly scalable. The event mechanism helps the server to respond in a non-blocking manner, unlike traditional servers which create limited threads to handle requests.

Built-in Libraries

Node.js comes with a rich set of built-in libraries that allow developers to handle various tasks such as file system operations, HTTP requests, and more without the need for external dependencies.

```
const os = require('os');

console.log('OS Platform:', os.platform());
console.log('OS CPU Architecture:', os.arch());
console.log('Total Memory:', os.totalmem());
console.log('Free Memory:', os.freemem());
```

Why Use Node.js for Building RESTful APIs?

Node.js offers several advantages for building RESTful APIs, making it a popular choice among developers:

- **High Performance:** Node.js's non-blocking I/O and event-driven architecture ensure high performance and responsiveness.

- **Scalability:** Its single-threaded nature powered by the event loop allows it to handle thousands of concurrent connections with minimal overhead.

- **JavaScript Everywhere:** Using JavaScript for both client-side and server-side development streamlines the development process and allows for code reuse.

- **Rich Ecosystem:** The Node Package Manager (npm) provides access to a vast library of open-source packages and modules, speeding up development and reducing the need to write boilerplate code.

Setting Up Node.js

To start working with Node.js, you need to install it on your local development environment. Follow these steps to set up Node.js:

1. **Download Node.js:** Visit https://nodejs.org/ and download the latest stable version of Node.js for your operating system.

2. **Install Node.js:** Run the installer and follow the instructions to complete the installation. You can verify the installation by running the following commands in your terminal:

    node -v
    npm -v

    These commands should display the installed versions of Node.js and npm, respectively.

3. **Initialize a Node.js Project:** Create a new directory for your project and navigate into it. Initialize your project with the following command:

    npm init -y

    This command generates a package.json file that keeps track of your project's dependencies and metadata.

With Node.js installed and your project initialized, you are now ready to start building RESTful APIs. In the upcoming chapters, we will delve deeper into setting up your development environment, understanding REST principles, and building scalable RESTful APIs using Node.js and various tools and libraries.

1.4 Tools and Setup

To build powerful and efficient RESTful APIs with Node.js, the right set of tools and a properly configured setup are crucial. This subchapter will guide you through the essential tools required and how to set up your development environment.

Node.js and npm

First and foremost, you'll need Node.js and npm (Node Package Manager). Node.js is a JavaScript runtime built on Chrome's V8 engine, and npm comes bundled with it. To check if Node.js and npm are already installed on your system, you can run the following commands in your terminal:

```
node -v
npm -v
```

If these commands return version numbers, Node.js and npm are already installed. If not, download and install Node.js from the official website: https://nodejs.org/. This installer includes npm.

Installing Visual Studio Code

A good code editor can significantly improve your productivity. Visual Studio Code (VS Code) is a popular, lightweight, yet powerful source code editor. It supports JavaScript out of the box and has an array of extensions available.

To install Visual Studio Code, download it from the official website: https://code.visualstudio.com/. Follow the installation instructions provided on the site.

Essential VS Code Extensions

Once Visual Studio Code is installed, you can further enhance its capabilities with a few essential extensions:

1. **Node.js Extension Pack**: This helps with Node.js development by adding relevant snippets and utilities.
2. **ESLint**: Automatically highlights and corrects JavaScript code quality issues based on the ESLint standard rules.
3. **Prettier**: An opinionated code formatter that enforces a consistent style throughout your codebase.

To fetch and install an extension, click the "Extensions" view icon on the Sidebar or press Ctrl+Shift+X, then search and install:

```
Node.js Extension Pack
ESLint
Prettier
```

Postman for API Testing

Postman is an essential tool for testing RESTful APIs. It provides a user-friendly interface to make HTTP requests and examine responses without writing a single line of code.

Download Postman from: https://www.postman.com/downloads/. Install it and get familiar with its interface as it's going to be handy when testing the endpoints of your API.

Setting Up a Project Folder

To keep your work organized, create a dedicated folder for your project. You can name it something meaningful, such as node-rest-api.

```
mkdir node-rest-api
cd node-rest-api
```

Initializing a Node.js Project

Within your project folder, initialize a new Node.js project with the following command:

```
npm init -y
```

This command creates a `package.json` file that tracks your project's dependencies and scripts. The `-y` flag generates a default `package.json` file without prompting you for any additional information.

Installing Essential Packages

Next, install the essential Node.js packages required to build your RESTful API. These include Express (a web framework for Node.js), body-parser (to parse incoming request bodies), and others as you need them.

```
npm install express body-parser
```

You can verify the installation by checking the `dependencies` section in your `package.json` file:

```
{
  "dependencies": {
    "express": "^x.x.x",
    "body-parser": "^x.x.x"
  }
}
```

Setting Up nodemon for Auto-restarts

For a smoother development workflow, use nodemon. It automatically restarts the server whenever you make code changes, saving you from manually stopping and starting the server.

Install nodemon globally with:

```
npm install -g nodemon
```

First Basic Express Server

To ensure everything is set up correctly, let's create a simple server. Create a file named server.js in your project folder and add the following code:

```
const express = require('express');
const app = express();
const port = 3000;

app.get('/', (req, res) => {
  res.send('Hello World!');
});

app.listen(port, () => {
  console.log(`Server is running on http://localhost:${port}`);
});
```

To run the server using nodemon, execute:

```
nodemon server.js
```

Navigate to http://localhost:3000 in your web browser, and you should see "Hello World!" displayed.

Conclusion

With Node.js, npm, Visual Studio Code, essential extensions, Postman, and nodemon, your environment is now set up to start building RESTful APIs. This setup will facilitate a seamless development process, enabling you to focus on writing efficient and scalable APIs with Node.js.

2. Understanding REST

2.1 Introduction to REST

Representational State Transfer (REST) has become the de facto standard for designing networked applications and APIs. RESTful services are a crucial part of web development, allowing developers to create scalable and maintainable systems that facilitate interaction between clients and servers over the internet.

What is REST?

REST is an architectural style that defines a set of constraints and properties based on HTTP. RESTful systems leverage these constraints to apply a consistent and reliable interface for communication. The term REST was introduced by Roy Fielding in his doctoral dissertation in 2000 and has since influenced many of the modern web service interfaces.

The main idea behind REST is to create systems that are interoperable, use standard HTTP methods, and communicate statelessly. RESTful services aim to provide:

1. **Performance**: By leveraging caches and consistent URLs, REST can improve performance.
2. **Scalability**: RESTful systems can be scaled by distributing the load across multiple servers.
3. **Simplicity**: Adopting REST encourages clear and intuitive interface designs.

Key Concepts of REST

To fully understand REST, it's essential to familiarize yourself with its core concepts:

Resources

Resources are the building blocks of RESTful services and can represent any data or object that the server can manage. Each resource is identified by a unique URL, referred to as a resource identifier.

For example, consider a simple RESTful service for managing books in a library. Each book can be represented as a resource with its own URL:

```
http://api.example.com/books/{id}
```

Here, {id} is a placeholder for the unique identifier of a specific book.

Representations

A representation of a resource is typically a JSON or XML document that encapsulates the current state or data of the resource. When a client requests a resource, the server sends back a representation of the resource:

```
GET http://api.example.com/books/1
```

Response:

```
{
  "id": 1,
  "title": "Effective JavaScript",
  "author": "David Herman",
  "publishedYear": 2012
}
```

Stateless Communication

One of the core principles of REST is stateless communication. Each request from a client to a server must contain all the information the server needs to fulfill that request. The server does not keep track of any client state between requests.

Here is an example of how a stateless request might look:

```
POST http://api.example.com/login
Content-Type: application/json

{
   "username": "exampleUser",
   "password": "securePassword"
}
```

The server processes this request independently without relying on any previous interactions.

URIs and Uniform Interface

Uniform Resource Identifiers (URIs) are used to uniquely identify and access resources. The uniform interface constraint ensures that all interactions with resources are done using a standard set of methods and conventions.

Consider these examples of standardized URIs and methods:

```
GET http://api.example.com/books - Retrieves a list of book
s
POST http://api.example.com/books - Creates a new book
GET http://api.example.com/books/{id} - Retrieves a specifi
c book by id
PUT http://api.example.com/books/{id} - Updates a specific
book by id
DELETE http://api.example.com/books/{id} - Deletes a specif
ic book by id
```

These methods directly map to CRUD (Create, Read, Update, Delete) operations, providing a clear and consistent way to interact with the API.

Why Use REST?

RESTful APIs offer numerous benefits, from scalability and performance to simplicity and compatibility. Some key advantages include:

- **Statelessness** simplifies server design and improves resilience.
- **Cacheability** improves performance and reduces server load.
- **Layered System** allows for a scalable and modular system architecture.
- **Uniform Interface** ensures a consistent and intuitive API design.

As we continue through this chapter, we'll delve deeper into the principles of REST, explore the various HTTP methods used in RESTful services, and learn best practices for designing robust and efficient RESTful APIs.

2.2 REST Principles

Representational State Transfer (REST) is an architectural style that outlines a set of principles and constraints for building web services. These principles are designed to facilitate scalable, stateless interactions between clients and servers. In this subchapter, we will explore the core principles of REST and how they guide the design and implementation of RESTful APIs. Understanding these principles will help you create APIs that are efficient, maintainable, and easy to use.

Statelessness

One of the fundamental principles of REST is statelessness. Each client request to the server must contain all the information the server needs to fulfill that request. The server should not store any client context between requests. This means that every request from a client must be understood and processed by the server in isolation.

Example:

```
GET /api/users/123 HTTP/1.1
Host: example.com
Authorization: Bearer your_token
```

In this example, the request contains an authorization token that allows the server to authenticate the client without having to store any session state.

Client-Server Separation

Another key principle of REST is the separation between the client and the server. The client is responsible for the user interface and user experience, while the server is responsible for data storage and business logic. This separation allows both the client and the server to evolve independently.

Client Request Example:

```
GET /api/products HTTP/1.1
Host: example.com
Accept: application/json
```

Server Response Example:

```
HTTP/1.1 200 OK
Content-Type: application/json

[
  {
    "id": 1,
    "name": "Product A",
    "price": 29.99
  },
  {
    "id": 2,
    "name": "Product B",
    "price": 49.99
  }
]
```

In this example, the client requests a list of products, and the server responds with the requested data in JSON format. The client can independently process and display this data.

Uniform Interface

The principle of a uniform interface simplifies and decouples the architecture, which enables each part to evolve independently. A uniform interface has several guiding constraints:

- **Resource Identification:** Resources are identified in requests using URIs. For example, `/api/users/123` identifies a specific user.

- **Resource Manipulation through Representations:** Clients interact with resources by sending representations, such as JSON or XML, that contain the data to be processed.

- **Self-descriptive Messages:** Each message contains enough information to describe how to process the message.

- **Hypermedia as the Engine of Application State (HATEOAS):** Clients interact with the application solely through hypermedia provided dynamically by application servers.

Example:

```
GET /api/articles HTTP/1.1
Host: example.com
Accept: application/json
```

Response:

```
{
  "articles": [
    {
      "id": 1,
      "title": "REST Principles",
      "links": {
        "self": "http://example.com/api/articles/1"
      }
    },
    {
      "id": 2,
      "title": "Understanding REST",
      "links": {
        "self": "http://example.com/api/articles/2"
      }
    }
  ]
}
```

In this example, the server provides URIs for each article in the response. Clients can use these URIs to interact with individual resources.

Cacheability

Responses from the server should explicitly indicate whether or not they are cacheable. Caching can reduce the client-server interaction, improve scalability, and enhance performance. HTTP provides several mechanisms for caching, including headers such as `Cache-Control`, `ETag`, and `Expires`.

Example:

```
GET /api/posts HTTP/1.1
Host: example.com
```

Response:

```
HTTP/1.1 200 OK
Content-Type: application/json
Cache-Control: max-age=3600

[
  {
    "id": 1,
    "title": "Introduction to Node.js",
    "content": "Node.js is a JavaScript runtime..."
  },
  {
    "id": 2,
    "title": "Building RESTful APIs",
    "content": "RESTful APIs are defined by..."
  }
]
```

In this response, the Cache-Control header tells the client to cache the response for 3600 seconds (1 hour).

Layered System

A layered system architecture allows an application to be composed of hierarchical layers by constraining component behavior. Each layer in the architecture has specific functions and responsibilities, such as load-balancing, authentication, and data storage. Components in a layer interact only with the adjacent layers.

Example:

1. **Client Layer:** Sends requests to the server.

2. **Application Layer:** Processes requests, performs business logic, and generates the appropriate responses.

3. **Database Layer:** Stores and retrieves data as needed.

Code on Demand (Optional)

One optional REST principle is code on demand. With this principle, servers can extend client functionality by transferring executable code. This is not commonly used but can be beneficial in specific scenarios, such as delivering client-side scripts.

Example:

```
GET /api/script HTTP/1.1
Host: example.com
```

Response:

```
HTTP/1.1 200 OK
Content-Type: application/javascript

(function() {
  console.log('Executing script from server.');
})();
```

In this example, the server provides a JavaScript snippet that the client can execute.

Understanding these principles is crucial for designing and building robust RESTful APIs. The next subchapter will delve into the HTTP methods that play a significant role in RESTful services.

2.3 HTTP Methods for RESTful Services

In this subchapter, we delve into the HTTP methods that form the backbone of RESTful services. These methods, often referred to as "verbs", perform various operations on the resources represented by URIs (Uniform Resource Identifiers). Understanding these methods is crucial for building RESTful APIs using Node.js.

GET: Retrieve Data

The GET method is used to retrieve data from the server. When a client invokes a GET request, it expects the server to return the requested resource without causing any side effects. This makes GET requests idempotent and safe.

Example:

Suppose you have an API for a book collection. To get a list of all books, you might use the following endpoint:

```
GET http://example.com/api/books
```

Sample code for handling a GET request in a Node.js server using Express:

```
app.get('/api/books', (req, res) => {
  const books = [
    { id: 1, title: "1984", author: "George Orwell" },
    { id: 2, title: "To Kill a Mockingbird", author: "Harpe
r Lee" }
  ];
  res.json(books);
});
```

POST: Create Data

The POST method is employed to create new resources on the server. When a client sends a POST request, it usually includes data to be added as a new resource.

Example:

To add a new book to the collection, you might use:

```
POST http://example.com/api/books
```

Sample code for handling a POST request:

```
app.post('/api/books', (req, res) => {
  const newBook = req.body; // Expecting a JSON body in the
format { title: "Book title", author: "Author name" }
  newBook.id = Date.now(); // Generate a unique ID
  // You would typically save the newBook to the database h
ere
  res.status(201).json(newBook);
});
```

PUT: Update Data

The PUT method is used to update an existing resource. It replaces the current representation of the resource with the given data.

Example:

To update the details of a book with id 1:

```
PUT http://example.com/api/books/1
```

Sample code for handling a PUT request:

```
app.put('/api/books/:id', (req, res) => {
  const bookId = req.params.id;
  const updatedBookData = req.body; // Expecting a JSON bod
y with updated book details
  // Update operation would occur here, e.g., finding the b
ook by ID and updating it in the database
  res.json({ id: bookId, ...updatedBookData });
});
```

DELETE: Remove Data

The DELETE method deletes the specified resource from the server.

Example:

To delete a book with id 1:

```{ DELETE http://example.com/api/books/1

Sample code for handling a DELETE request:

```javascript
app.delete('/api/books/:id', (req, res) => {
  const bookId = req.params.id;
  // The delete operation would happen here, such as removi
ng the book from the database
  res.status(204).send(); // 204 No Content status code ind
icates successful deletion
});
```

PATCH: Modify Data

The PATCH method applies partial modifications to a resource, rather than replacing the entire resource as with PUT.

Example:

To update just the title of a book with id 1:
```

```
PATCH http://example.com/api/books/1
```

Sample code for handling a PATCH request:

```
app.patch('/api/books/:id', (req, res) => {
  const bookId = req.params.id;
  const updatedData = req.body; // Expecting a JSON body wi
th fields to be updated
  // Apply the partial update to the book in the database h
ere
  res.json({ id: bookId, ...updatedData });
});
```

Conclusion

Understanding and properly implementing these HTTP methods is essential for creating robust and RESTful APIs. Each method serves a specific purpose and ensures that your API adheres to REST principles, allowing it to be intuitive and predictable to clients.

2.4 Designing RESTful APIs

Designing RESTful APIs is an essential skill for building robust and scalable web services. This subchapter will cover the best practices for creating RESTful APIs, ensuring that your services are easy to use, maintain, and extend. We'll discuss crucial aspects of API design like resource identification, URI structuring, standardizing HTTP methods, status codes, pagination, and versioning.

Resource Identification

Resources are the heart of RESTful APIs. It's crucial to identify what resources your API will expose. Each resource should represent a distinct entity, such as a user, a blog post, or a product. Resources are typically identified and manipulated using Uniform Resource Identifiers (URIs).

For example, to represent a collection of users and a single user, you might use:

- Collection URI: `https://api.example.com/users`
- Individual Resource URI:
  `https://api.example.com/users/{userId}`

URI Structuring

A well-structured URI helps consumers of your API understand the organization of your resources:

- Use nouns to represent resources:
- Avoid using verbs in URIs — HTTP methods should convey the action.
- Employ a hierarchical, clear, and predictable structure.

Examples of properly structured URIs:

- Collection of resources:
  `https://api.example.com/products`
- Single resource within a collection:
  `https://api.example.com/products/12345`

Standardizing HTTP Methods

HTTP methods define how you can manipulate resources in your API. The primary methods used in RESTful design are:

- GET for retrieving resources.
- POST for creating resources.
- PUT or PATCH for updating resources.
- DELETE for removing resources.

Example of a GET request to retrieve a list of users:

```
GET https://api.example.com/users
```

Example of a POST request to create a new user:

```
POST https://api.example.com/users
Content-Type: application/json

{
  "name": "John Doe",
  "email": "john.doe@example.com"
}
```

Status Codes

HTTP status codes communicate the outcome of an HTTP request. Commonly used status codes in RESTful APIs are:

- 200 OK: The request was successful.

- **201 Created**: The resource was successfully created (usually in response to POST requests).

- **204 No Content**: The request was successful, but there is no content to return.

- **400 Bad Request**: The request was invalid.

- **401 Unauthorized**: Authentication is required.

- **404 Not Found**: The requested resource could not be found.

- **500 Internal Server Error**: A generic error message for unexpected server issues.

Example of a successful GET request response with status **200 OK**:

```
HTTP/1.1 200 OK
Content-Type: application/json

[
  {
    "id": 1,
    "name": "John Doe",
    "email": "john.doe@example.com"
  },
  {
    "id": 2,
    "name": "Jane Smith",
    "email": "jane.smith@example.com"
  }
]
```

Pagination

For endpoints that return large lists of items, it is advisable to implement pagination to manage performance and usability. Common pagination strategies include `limit` and `offset`.

Example of a paginated GET request:

```
GET https://api.example.com/products?limit=10&offset=20
```

- `limit` specifies the number of items to return.
- `offset` specifies the starting point for returning items.

Versioning

APIs evolve, and introducing breaking changes without affecting existing clients is vital. Versioning your API helps manage changes gracefully. Common versioning strategies include:

- URI Versioning: `https://api.example.com/v1/users`
- Header Versioning: `GET https://api.example.com/users` with a custom header (e.g., `Accept: application/vnd.example.v1+json`)

Example API Design

Here's a simplified example of how a user-related RESTful API might be designed:

- Retrieve all users:

  ```
  GET https://api.example.com/v1/users
  ```

- Retrieve a specific user:

  ```
  GET https://api.example.com/v1/users/{userId}
  ```

- Create a new user:

  ```
  POST https://api.example.com/v1/users
  Content-Type: application/json

  {
    "name": "Alice Johnson",
    "email": "alice.johnson@example.com"
  }
  ```

- Update an existing user:

```
PUT https://api.example.com/v1/users/{userId}
Content-Type: application/json

{
  "name": "Alice Johnson",
  "email": "alice.johnson@newdomain.com"
}
```

- Delete a user:

```
DELETE https://api.example.com/v1/users/{userId}
```

By following these principles and examples, you can create well-designed RESTful APIs that are intuitive, scalable, and easy to maintain. This is essential for effective integration and long-term success of your API ecosystem.

3. Setting Up Your Environment

3.1 Installing Node.js and NPM

In order to build RESTful APIs with Node.js, you first need to set up your development environment by installing Node.js and NPM (Node Package Manager). Node.js provides the runtime environment for executing JavaScript code outside the browser, while NPM is the default package manager for Node.js, allowing you to manage dependencies for your project seamlessly. This subchapter will guide you through the process of installing Node.js and NPM on various operating systems.

Installing on Windows

1. **Download Node.js Installer:**

   Visit the official Node.js website https://nodejs.org/ and click on the "LTS" (Long Term Support) version to download the installer.

2. **Run the Installer:**

   Open the downloaded .msi file and follow the installation steps. Make sure to check the box that says "Automatically install the necessary tools" during the installation process.

3. **Verify Installation:**

   To verify the installation, open Command Prompt or PowerShell and type the following commands:

   ```
   node -v
   ```

   ```
   npm -v
   ```

   You should see the version numbers for Node.js and NPM, indicating that both are installed correctly.

Installing on macOS

1. **Download Node.js Installer:**

   Visit https://nodejs.org/ and download the "LTS" version for macOS.

2. **Run the Installer:**

   Open the downloaded `.pkg` file and follow the installation steps.

3. **Verify Installation:**

   Open Terminal and type the following commands:

   ```
   node -v
   npm -v
   ```

   You should see the version numbers for Node.js and NPM.

Installing on Ubuntu/Debian Linux

1. **Update Package Index:**

   Open Terminal and update the package index by running:

   ```
   sudo apt update
   ```

2. **Install Node.js and NPM:**

   Install Node.js from the NodeSource repository for more recent version availability:

   ```
   curl -sL https://deb.nodesource.com/setup_lts.x | sud
   o -E bash -
   sudo apt install -y nodejs
   ```

3. **Verify Installation:**

   Verify the installation by running the following commands:

   ```
   node -v
   ```

```
npm -v
```

You should see the version numbers for Node.js and NPM.

Installing on CentOS/RHEL/Fedora

1. **Add NodeSource Repository:**

   Open Terminal and add the NodeSource repository for a stable Node.js version:

   ```
   curl -sL https://rpm.nodesource.com/setup_lts.x | sud
   o bash -
   ```

2. **Install Node.js and NPM:**

   Install Node.js and NPM by running:

   ```
   sudo yum install -y nodejs
   ```

3. **Verify Installation:**

   Verify the installation by running:

   ```
   node -v
   ```

   ```
   npm -v
   ```

   You should see the version numbers for Node.js and NPM.

Updating NPM

Once Node.js and NPM are installed, it's good practice to update NPM to the latest version:

```
npm install -g npm@latest
```

Conclusion

By following these steps, you've installed Node.js and NPM on your system, and you're now ready to start building RESTful APIs. In the next subchapter, you'll learn how to set up a project directory, which will serve as your workspace for developing Node.js applications.

3.2 Setting Up a Project Directory

When building a RESTful API with Node.js, setting up an organized project directory is crucial for maintaining clarity and ease of development. In this section, we'll go through the steps needed to create a structured project directory that will help you manage your code efficiently.

Creating the Project Directory

First, create a new directory for your project. You can name it anything you like, but for our example, we'll call it my-restful-api.

Open your terminal and run the following commands:

```
mkdir my-restful-api
cd my-restful-api
```

Initializing the Project

Once inside your project directory, initialize it as a Node.js project using npm. This will create a package.json file that will hold various metadata relevant to the project.

Run the following command:

```
npm init -y
```

The -y flag automatically answers "yes" to all prompts, using the default settings to create the package.json file.

Directory Structure

Creating a well-structured directory layout is essential for keeping your project maintainable. Here's a recommended basic structure for a Node.js RESTful API project:

```
my-restful-api/
├── node_modules/
├── src/
│   ├── controllers/
│   ├── models/
│   ├── routes/
│   ├── index.js
├── .env
├── .gitignore
├── package.json
├── README.md
```

Creating Subdirectories

Let's go ahead and create these subdirectories and an initial file in your project:

```
mkdir -p src/controllers src/models src/routes
touch src/index.js .env .gitignore README.md
```

Explanation of Each Element

1. **node_modules/**: This directory contains all the npm packages your project depends on. It gets generated when you run npm install.

2. **src/**: This is the main directory where your application code will reside.

   o **controllers/**: This directory will hold all the controller files. Each controller typically corresponds to one or more routes and contains the business logic of your application.

o **models/**: This directory will contain the model files representing the data structures. If you're using an ORM like Sequelize or Mongoose, the models will be defined here.

o **routes/**: This directory will store all the route definitions. Each file typically represents a group of related routes.

3. **src/index.js**: This file will act as the main entry point for your application.

4. **.env**: This file will store your environment variables. Make sure it is added to your `.gitignore` to keep sensitive data out of your version control system.

5. **.gitignore**: This file tells git which files and directories to ignore, helping to keep your repository clean. You can add common items to ignore, such as `node_modules/` and `.env`.

   Example `.gitignore` file:

   ```
   node_modules/
   .env
   ```

6. **package.json**: This file contains metadata about your project, including dependencies, scripts, and version information. It was created when you ran `npm init -y`.

7. **README.md**: This file provides an overview and documentation for your project.

Final Steps

With everything in place, let's install some essential packages that we'll need later in this book. Run the following command to install Express.js, a minimalist web framework for Node.js:

```
npm install express
```

Having completed these steps, you now have a well-structured project directory ready for developing a RESTful API with Node.js. In the next sections, we'll dive deeper into configuring environment variables and installing additional essential packages.

3.3 Configuring Environment Variables

Environment variables play a crucial role in configuring various aspects of your Node.js application without hardcoding values directly into your source code. They allow you to maintain flexibility and security, especially when dealing with sensitive data such as API keys, database credentials, and configuration settings.

What are Environment Variables?

Environment variables are key-value pairs managed outside the source code of your application. They can be set in different ways, such as within your development environment, on a server, or through a .env file. These variables are accessible within your Node.js application using process.env.

Here's an example of accessing environment variables in Node.js:

```
console.log(process.env.MY_VARIABLE);
```

Using .env Files

A common practice for managing environment variables in Node.js applications is using a .env file. This file usually resides in the root directory of your project and contains key-value pairs, one per line:

```
PORT=3000
DB_HOST=localhost
DB_USER=root
DB_PASS=s1mpl3
```

To make use of these variables within your Node.js code, you'll need a package like dotenv. The dotenv package loads environment variables from a .env file into process.env.

Installing `dotenv`

First, install the `dotenv` package using NPM:

```
npm install dotenv
```

Loading Environment Variables

Next, import and configure `dotenv` at the top of your entry file (e.g., `app.js`):

```
require('dotenv').config();
```

This will read your `.env` file and make the variables available in `process.env`:

```
console.log(process.env.DB_HOST); // localhost
console.log(process.env.DB_USER); // root
```

Setting Environment Variables in Different Environments

Development

For development purposes, setting up a `.env` file as described above is usually sufficient.

Production

In a production environment, you generally don't want to use a `.env` file. Instead, you should set environment variables on the server directly. How you do this will depend on your hosting platform. For example, on a Unix-based server, you can set environment variables directly in the shell:

```
export PORT=8080
export DB_HOST=prod-db-server
export DB_USER=admin
export DB_PASS=secureP@ss
```

Accessing Environment Variables in Your Application

You can now access these variables throughout your Node.js application using `process.env`. Here's an example of using environment variables to configure a database connection:

```
const mysql = require('mysql');

const connection = mysql.createConnection({
    host: process.env.DB_HOST,
    user: process.env.DB_USER,
    password: process.env.DB_PASS,
});

connection.connect(err => {
    if (err) {
        console.error('Error connecting to the database:',
err);
        return;
    }
    console.log('Connected to the database');
});

connection.end();
```

Best Practices

1. **Never Hardcode Sensitive Information**: Always use environment variables to store sensitive information.

2. **Use a .env.example File**: Commit a `.env.example` file to your version control system to provide a template for other developers.

3. **Validate Environment Variables**: Use packages like `joi` to validate the presence and correctness of required environment variables.

Example of validating environment variables:

```
const Joi = require('joi');

const envVarsSchema = Joi.object({
    PORT: Joi.number().required(),
    DB_HOST: Joi.string().required(),
    DB_USER: Joi.string().required(),
    DB_PASS: Joi.string().required(),
}).unknown().required();

const { error, value: envVars } = envVarsSchema.validate(process.env);

if (error) {
    throw new Error(`Config validation error: ${error.message}`);
}

const config = {
    port: envVars.PORT,
    db: {
        host: envVars.DB_HOST,
        user: envVars.DB_USER,
        pass: envVars.DB_PASS,
    },
};

module.exports = config;
```

By following these practices, you can ensure that your Node.js application remains flexible, secure, and maintainable.

3.4 Installing Essential Packages

Setting up the project environment involves installing several essential packages that will form the backbone of your RESTful API development. With Node.js and NPM (Node Package Manager) already installed, you are ready to proceed. This subchapter will guide you through installing fundamental packages that you will frequently utilize throughout the book.

Initializing the Project

Before installing packages, you must ensure that your project directory is initialized with a package.json file. If you haven't done this yet, navigate to your project directory and run:

```
npm init -y
```

This command generates a package.json file with default settings, which serves as the manifest for your Node.js project. You can customize this file later as needed.

Installing Express.js

Express.js is a minimal and flexible Node.js web application framework that provides a robust set of features for web and mobile applications. Start by installing Express.js:

```
npm install express
```

After installing, you can verify the installation by checking the dependencies section in your package.json file.

Installing Nodemon

Nodemon is a utility that monitors for any changes in your source code and automatically restarts your server. This tool is extremely useful during development. Install Nodemon as a development dependency:

```
npm install --save-dev nodemon
```

You can set up a script in `package.json` to use Nodemon:

```
"scripts": {
  "start": "nodemon index.js"
}
```

With this configuration, you can start your server using `npm start`, and Nodemon will handle the rest.

Installing dotenv

Environment variables are crucial for managing configuration settings and sensitive information securely. To load environment variables from a `.env` file into `process.env`, you'll use the `dotenv` package:

```
npm install dotenv
```

Create a `.env` file in your project's root directory:

```
PORT=3000
DATABASE_URL=mongodb://localhost:27017/mydatabase
```

Then, in your main server file, load the environment variables at the top:

```
require('dotenv').config();
const express = require('express');
const app = express();

// Your code here
```

Installing Body-Parser

To handle incoming request bodies in a middleware before your handlers, you will need the body-parser package:

```
npm install body-parser
```

Integrate body-parser into your Express application:

```
const bodyParser = require('body-parser');
app.use(bodyParser.json());
app.use(bodyParser.urlencoded({ extended: true }));
```

Installing Mongoose

If you are using MongoDB, Mongoose will be an essential ODM (Object Data Modeling) library. Install Mongoose with the following command:

```
npm install mongoose
```

After installing, you can set up a connection to your MongoDB in your server file:

```
const mongoose = require('mongoose');
mongoose.connect(process.env.DATABASE_URL, { useNewUrlParse
r: true, useUnifiedTopology: true })
  .then(() => console.log('MongoDB connected'))
  .catch(err => console.error('MongoDB connection error:',
err));
```

Summary

To summarize, the essential packages covered in this section include:

- Express.js for creating the server
- Nodemon for automatic server restarts during development
- dotenv for managing environment variables
- body-parser for parsing incoming request bodies
- Mongoose for interacting with MongoDB

With these packages installed and configured, you are now equipped with the foundational tools needed to build and run your RESTful API efficiently. The next steps will involve diving deeper into utilizing these packages to structure your API, handle routing, connect to a database, and implement various other features. Continue your journey with confidence, knowing that your development environment is properly set up.

4. Introduction to Node.js

4.1 What is Node.js?

Node.js is a powerful and versatile JavaScript runtime built on Chrome's V8 JavaScript engine. It enables developers to build scalable, high-performance applications by executing JavaScript code outside a browser environment. Traditionally, JavaScript was confined to the client side, running only within web browsers, but Node.js extended its reach to the server side, revolutionizing how web applications and network services are developed.

Why Node.js?

The core philosophy of Node.js is to provide an efficient environment for building I/O-bound applications. Its non-blocking, event-driven architecture allows it to handle multiple operations simultaneously, making it ideal for applications that require real-time interaction, such as chat applications, gaming servers, and APIs.

Node.js has several features that make it an excellent choice for building RESTful APIs:

- **Non-blocking I/O**: Node.js uses an event-driven, non-blocking I/O model, which makes it lightweight and efficient. This is particularly useful for handling multiple concurrent operations.

- **Single Programming Language**: With Node.js, you can use JavaScript for both frontend and backend development, which creates a seamless development experience.

- **NPM Ecosystem**: Node Package Manager (NPM) offers a vast repository of libraries and modules that you can easily integrate into your applications, saving time and effort.

- **High Performance**: Thanks to its modern and optimized V8 engine, Node.js executes JavaScript code with impressive speed and efficiency.

Hello World in Node.js

To better understand what Node.js is and how it works, let's dive into a basic "Hello World" example. This simple server will respond with "Hello World" when accessed via a web browser or any HTTP client.

First, ensure you have Node.js installed on your machine. You can download it from https://nodejs.org/. Once installed, create a new file named app.js and insert the following code:

```javascript
// Import the built-in 'http' module
const http = require('http');

// Define the hostname and port number
const hostname = '127.0.0.1';
const port = 3000;

// Create a server that sends a "Hello World" response
const server = http.createServer((req, res) => {
  res.statusCode = 200;
  res.setHeader('Content-Type', 'text/plain');
  res.end('Hello World\n');
});

// Start the server and listen on the specified port and hostname
server.listen(port, hostname, () => {
  console.log(`Server running at http://${hostname}:${port}/`);
});
```

To run the server, navigate to the directory containing app.js and execute the following command in your terminal:

```
node app.js
```

Open your web browser and go to http://127.0.0.1:3000/. You should see "Hello World" displayed. This simple example illustrates how Node.js can create a web server and handle HTTP requests with just a few lines of code.

Core Modules in Node.js

Node.js comes with a variety of built-in modules that simplify the implementation of common tasks. Some key modules include:

- **HTTP**: Used to create HTTP servers and handle HTTP requests and responses.
- **FS**: Provides file system operations such as reading and writing files.
- **Path**: Helps manage and manipulate file paths.
- **Util**: Contains utility functions for debugging and inspecting objects.

Here's an example that demonstrates the use of the fs (file system) module to read a file asynchronously:

```
const fs = require('fs');

// Read the contents of a file asynchronously
fs.readFile('example.txt', 'utf8', (err, data) => {
  if (err) {
    console.error('Error reading file:', err);
    return;
  }
  console.log('File contents:', data);
});
```

By leveraging these core modules, Node.js simplifies many server-side programming tasks, enabling you to focus on building your application rather than dealing with low-level details.

Conclusion

Node.js offers a robust and efficient environment for building scalable server-side applications. Its non-blocking I/O, unified programming language, rich ecosystem, and high performance make it exceptionally well-suited for developing RESTful APIs. As we continue through this chapter, we'll explore how to set up Node.js, understand its architecture, and dive into some of its essential modules, laying a strong foundation for more advanced topics in the following chapters.

4.2 Setting Up Node.js

To start developing RESTful APIs with Node.js, you first need to set up the Node.js runtime environment on your local machine. This section will guide you step-by-step through the installation process, ensuring that you have all the required tools to begin your journey.

Installing Node.js

Downloading Node.js

Node.js can be downloaded from its official website. Visit the following URL to find the appropriate installer for your operating system:

```
https://nodejs.org/en/download/
```

Selecting the Version

On the download page, you will find two versions: LTS (Long Term Support) and the Current version. For most projects and especially for production environments, it is advisable to use the LTS version as it ensures stability and long-term support.

Installation on Windows

1. Download the Windows installer from the Node.js website.

2. Run the installer.

3. Follow the steps in the setup wizard. The default settings are sufficient for most users.

4. Confirm that Node.js and npm (Node Package Manager) have been installed correctly by running the following commands in your command prompt:

```
node -v
npm -v
```

Installation on macOS

1. Download the macOS installer from the Node.js website.

2. Open the .pkg file and run the installer.

3. Follow the prompts in the installer.

4. Confirm that Node.js and npm have been installed correctly by running the following commands in your Terminal:

```
node -v
npm -v
```

Installation on Linux

To install Node.js on Linux, you can use a package manager. For example, on Ubuntu, you can use apt:

1. Open your terminal.

2. Add the NodeSource APT repository for Node 14.x (LTS version):

```
curl -fsSL https://deb.nodesource.com/setup_14.x | sudo -E bash -
```

3. Install Node.js and npm:

```
sudo apt-get install -y nodejs
```

4. Verify the installation by checking the versions of Node.js and npm:

```
node -v
npm -v
```

NPM (Node Package Manager)

After installing Node.js, npm is installed automatically. npm helps in managing dependencies, libraries, and packages in your Node.js projects. You can use npm to install, update, and remove packages.

Installing Packages

To install a package globally, you can use the -g flag:

```
npm install -g <package-name>
```

To install a package locally and add it to your package.json file:

```
npm install <package-name> --save
```

Initializing a Node.js Project

To start a new Node.js project, you need to create a package.json file. This file contains metadata about your project and records dependencies that your project requires.

1. Create a new directory for your project and navigate into it:

   ```
   mkdir my-nodejs-app
   cd my-nodejs-app
   ```

2. Initialize a new Node.js project by generating a package.json file. You can do this interactively:

   ```
   npm init
   ```

   Follow the prompts to provide information about your project. You can also use npm init -y to create a package.json file with default values.

Verifying Your Setup

To ensure everything is set up correctly, you can create a simple Node.js script.

1. Create a new file named app.js in your project directory:

    ```
    touch app.js
    ```

2. Open app.js in your preferred text editor and add the following code:

    ```
    console.log('Node.js is successfully installed and ru
    nning!');
    ```

3. Run the script using Node.js:

    ```
    node app.js
    ```

You should see the output:

```
Node.js is successfully installed and running!
```

This confirms that your setup is complete and you are ready to start building RESTful APIs with Node.js.

4.3 Node.js Architecture

Node.js is a powerful and efficient runtime environment for executing JavaScript code server-side. Its architecture is designed to handle asynchronous events and I/O operations efficiently, which makes it particularly well-suited for building scalable network applications like RESTful APIs. In this section, we'll explore the key components and design principles of Node.js architecture to understand how it achieves high performance and scalability.

Event-Driven Architecture

Node.js uses an event-driven architecture, a paradigm in which the flow of the program is determined by events, such as user actions, I/O operations, or messages. This design enables Node.js to handle numerous concurrent connections without creating multiple threads, which is a common approach in traditional server-side applications.

Node.js leverages an event loop to process and manage these events. The event loop is a single-threaded loop that keeps track of asynchronous operations like reading from a file, making HTTP requests, or querying a database. When an event occurs, it is placed in the event queue, and the event loop picks it up for execution.

Here's a simple example to illustrate the event-driven nature of Node.js:

```
const fs = require('fs');

// Asynchronous file read
fs.readFile('example.txt', 'utf8', (err, data) => {
  if (err) throw err;
  console.log(data);
});

console.log('This will print first.');
```

In this example, the `fs.readFile` function initiates an asynchronous file read operation. While Node.js waits for the file read operation to complete, it continues executing other parts of the code. This allows Node.js to handle multiple tasks concurrently without blocking the main thread.

Non-Blocking I/O

A fundamental aspect of Node.js is its non-blocking I/O operations. Traditional I/O operations are blocking, meaning the thread executing the operation is halted until the operation completes. In contrast, non-blocking I/O allows other operations to continue processing while the I/O operation is being performed, thus improving overall efficiency.

This is achieved by using callbacks, promises, or asynchronous functions (using `async` and `await` keywords). Here's an example using an HTTP request:

```javascript
const https = require('https');

// Non-blocking HTTP request
https.get('https://api.example.com/data', (res) => {
  let data = '';

  // A chunk of data has been received.
  res.on('data', (chunk) => {
    data += chunk;
  });

  // The whole response has been received.
  res.on('end', () => {
    console.log(JSON.parse(data));
  });
}).on('error', (err) => {
  console.error('Error: ' + err.message);
});

console.log('HTTP request initiated.');
```

In this scenario, the HTTP request is made asynchronously. Node.js doesn't wait for the response from the server; instead, it continues executing subsequent lines of code. When data is received, an event is emitted, triggering the callback functions specified for 'data' and 'end' events.

Single-Threaded Event Loop

Despite being single-threaded, Node.js can handle thousands of simultaneous connections thanks to its efficient event loop. This might seem counterintuitive, but the single-threaded nature of the event loop simplifies concurrency management and avoids the overhead associated with creating and managing multiple threads.

The event loop follows a series of phases to process events:

1. **Timers**: Executes callbacks scheduled by `setTimeout()` and `setInterval()`.
2. **Pending Callbacks**: Executes I/O callbacks deferred to the next loop iteration.
3. **Idle, Prepare**: Internal use only.
4. **Poll**: Retrieves new I/O events and executes their callbacks.
5. **Check**: Executes callbacks scheduled by `setImmediate()`.
6. **Close Callbacks**: Executes `close` event callbacks, such as the `close` event of TCP servers.

Here's a simple example using `setTimeout` and `setImmediate`:

```
console.log('Start');

setTimeout(() => {
  console.log('Timeout callback');
}, 0);

setImmediate(() => {
  console.log('Immediate callback');
});

console.log('End');
```

Output:

```
Start
End
Immediate callback
Timeout callback
```

In this example, the setImmediate callback is executed before the setTimeout callback, even though both are scheduled to execute as soon as possible. This is because the event loop prioritizes immediate callbacks over timeout callbacks.

Asynchronous Programming Model

Node.js promotes an asynchronous programming model, reducing the time spent waiting for I/O operations to complete. This model is facilitated through callbacks, promises, and async/await syntax.

Callbacks

Callbacks are functions passed as arguments to other functions, called once an asynchronous operation completes. However, extensive use of callbacks can lead to callback hell or pyramid of doom, making code harder to read and maintain.

Example:

```
const fs = require('fs');

fs.readFile('example.txt', (err, data) => {
  if (err) console.error(err);
  else console.log(data);
});
```

Promises

Promises provide a cleaner way to handle asynchronous operations, representing the eventual completion or failure of an asynchronous task.

Example:

```
const fs = require('fs').promises;

fs.readFile('example.txt', 'utf8')
  .then(data => console.log(data))
  .catch(err => console.error(err));
```

Async/Await

Async/await is syntactic sugar built on promises, allowing asynchronous code to be written in a more synchronous manner.

Example:

```
const fs = require('fs').promises;

async function readFile() {
  try {
    const data = await fs.readFile('example.txt', 'utf8');
    console.log(data);
  } catch (err) {
    console.error(err);
  }
}

readFile();
```

Conclusion

Node.js architecture, with its event-driven and non-blocking I/O principles, empowers developers to build highly scalable and efficient server-side applications. Understanding these core concepts is crucial for leveraging Node.js to its full potential when building RESTful APIs.

4.4 Basic Node.js Modules

Node.js comes with a rich set of built-in modules that provide fundamental functionalities essential for creating a robust server-side application. These modules are a crucial part of the Node.js ecosystem and can be required in your application using the require function. This subchapter will introduce some of the most commonly used Node.js modules and provide examples of their usage.

File System (fs) Module

The fs module allows you to interact with the file system in a way modeled on standard POSIX functions. This module provides both synchronous and asynchronous methods for file operations.

Reading a File

To read a file asynchronously, you can use the fs.readFile method:

```
const fs = require('fs');

fs.readFile('example.txt', 'utf8', (err, data) => {
    if (err) {
        console.error('Error reading the file:', err);
        return;
    }
    console.log('File contents:', data);
});
```

Writing to a File

To write data to a file asynchronously, you can use the fs.writeFile method:

```
const fs = require('fs');

const data = 'Hello, this is a sample text.';

fs.writeFile('output.txt', data, (err) => {
    if (err) {
        console.error('Error writing the file:', err);
        return;
    }
    console.log('File written successfully');
});
```

HTTP Module

The http module allows you to create an HTTP server and client. This is a core module that's vital for building web servers and HTTP clients in Node.js.

Creating a Basic HTTP Server

Here is an example of how to create a simple HTTP server that responds with "Hello, World!" to every request:

```
const http = require('http');

const server = http.createServer((req, res) => {
    res.statusCode = 200;
    res.setHeader('Content-Type', 'text/plain');
    res.end('Hello, World!\n');
});

const PORT = 3000;
server.listen(PORT, () => {
    console.log(`Server running at http://localhost:${PORT}
/`);
});
```

Path Module

The `path` module provides utilities for working with file and directory paths. It is especially useful for handling and transforming file paths in a more platform-independent manner.

Joining Paths

You can use the `path.join` method to combine multiple path segments into a single path:

```
const path = require('path');

const joinedPath = path.join('/foo', 'bar', 'baz/asdf', 'qu
ux', '..');
console.log('Joined Path:', joinedPath);   // Output: /foo/b
ar/baz/asdf
```

Resolving Absolute Paths

To resolve a sequence of path segments into an absolute path, use the `path.resolve` method:

```
const path = require('path');

const absolutePath = path.resolve('foo/bar', '/tmp/file/',
'..', 'a/../subfile');
console.log('Resolved Path:', absolutePath);   // Output on
Unix: /tmp/subfile
```

URL Module

The `url` module provides utilities for URL resolution and parsing. It is handy for handling and normalizing URLs in your Node.js applications.

Parsing a URL

To parse a URL string into an object, you can use the `url.parse` method:

```
const url = require('url');

const parsedUrl = url.parse('http://www.example.com:8080/pa
th/name?query=1#hash');
console.log('Parsed URL:', parsedUrl);
```

Formatting a URL

To construct a URL string from an object, use the `url.format` method:

```
const url = require('url');

const formattedUrl = url.format({
    protocol: 'http',
    hostname: 'www.example.com',
    port: 8080,
    pathname: '/path/name',
    query: { query: 1 },
    hash: '#hash'
});
console.log('Formatted URL:', formattedUrl);
```

OS Module

The `os` module provides a few basic operating-system-related utility functions. It provides information about the computer operating system.

Retrieving System Information

You can use the `os` module to fetch details like the system's hostname, platform, and architecture:

```
const os = require('os');

console.log('OS Hostname:', os.hostname());
console.log('OS Platform:', os.platform());
console.log('OS Architecture:', os.arch());
```

Events Module

The events module allows you to work with events and event-driven programming. EventEmitter class is key to this module and can be used to handle custom events.

Creating and Listening to Events

You can create an instance of EventEmitter and listen to as well as emit events:

```
const EventEmitter = require('events');

class MyEmitter extends EventEmitter {}

const myEmitter = new MyEmitter();

myEmitter.on('event', () => {
    console.log('An event occurred!');
});

myEmitter.emit('event');
```

These modules form the backbone of many Node.js applications. Understanding these basics will enable you to build more complex functionality as you proceed with developing your RESTful APIs.

5. Building a Basic Server

5.1 Setting Up Your Development Environment

Before diving into building your first basic web server with Node.js, it's crucial to set up your development environment correctly. This chapter will guide you through the necessary steps to get your environment ready, ensuring you can develop and run your Node.js applications seamlessly.

Installing Node.js

First and foremost, you need to install Node.js, which also includes npm (Node Package Manager), a tool that helps you manage libraries and packages for your Node.js applications.

1. **Download Node.js**: Visit the official Node.js website at `https://nodejs.org/` and download the latest stable version suitable for your operating system (Windows, macOS, or Linux).

2. **Install Node.js**: Run the installer and follow the on-screen instructions. Ensure that you install both Node.js and npm.

3. **Verify Installation**: After installation, open your terminal or command prompt and type the following commands to check the versions installed:

```
node -v
npm -v
```

If both commands return version numbers, your installation is successful.

Setting Up a Project Directory

Next, you need to set up a dedicated directory for your project. This directory will contain all the files and configurations necessary for your Node.js server.

1. **Create a Directory**: Open your terminal and create a new directory named basic-server-project (or any name of your choice):

```
mkdir basic-server-project
cd basic-server-project
```

2. **Initialize npm**: Within the project directory, initialize npm to create a package.json file. This file will manage your project's dependencies and scripts.

```
npm init -y
```

Initialization with the -y flag automatically fills out the package.json with default values.

Installing Essential Packages

To build a Node.js server efficiently, you need to install a few basic packages.

1. **Express.js**: Express is a minimal and flexible Node.js web application framework that provides a robust set of features for web and mobile applications.

```
npm install express
```

3. **Nodemon (Optional)**: Nodemon is a utility that monitors for any changes in your source and automatically restarts your server. It's extremely helpful during development.

```
npm install --save-dev nodemon
```

Setting Up Scripts

You can configure scripts in `package.json` to simplify the process of starting your server during development. Open `package.json` and add the following under the `"scripts"` section:

```
"scripts": {
  "start": "node index.js",
  "dev": "nodemon index.js"
}
```

- The `start` script runs the server using Node.js.
- The `dev` script runs the server using nodemon, ensuring it restarts automatically when it detects file changes.

Creating Your Main Application File

With everything set up, the next step is to create the main file for your server.

1. **Create `index.js`**: In your project directory, create a file named `index.js`.

```
touch index.js
```

4. **Write Basic Code**: Open `index.js` in your preferred text editor and add the following basic server configuration code:

```
const express = require('express');
const app = express();

const PORT = process.env.PORT || 3000;

app.get('/', (req, res) => {
  res.send('Hello, World!');
});

app.listen(PORT, () => {
  console.log(`Server is running on http://localhost:${PORT}`);
});
```

Running Your Server

Now that everything is set up and you have a basic server file in place, you can run your server.

1. **Start the Server**: In your terminal, start the server by running either of the following commands:

```
npm start
```

or, for development with auto-restart,

```
npm run dev
```

5. **Access the Server**: Open your web browser and navigate to `http://localhost:3000`. You should see the message "Hello, World!" displayed.

Congratulations! Your development environment is now ready, and you have a basic Node.js server running. In the next subchapter, you'll learn how to write more complex server logic and handle different routes and requests.

5.2 Writing Your First Node.js Server

In this subchapter, we will guide you through the process of creating your first Node.js server from scratch. You will learn how to initialize a Node.js project, set up a basic server, and test your server to ensure it is running correctly.

Initializing a Node.js Project

Before writing any code, you need to initialize a new Node.js project. This step involves creating a `package.json` file, which contains metadata about the project and its dependencies.

1. Open your terminal or command prompt.

2. Navigate to the directory where you want to create your project.

3. Run the following command to initialize a new Node.js project:

   ```
   npm init -y
   ```

   The `-y` flag will automatically answer "yes" to all prompts and create a `package.json` file with default settings.

Installing Required Packages

For our basic server, we do not need any additional packages. The built-in `http` module in Node.js will suffice for our purposes.

Creating the Server File

You can now create a file for your server. Let's name it `server.js`.

1. In your project directory, create a new file named `server.js`.
2. Open `server.js` in your favorite text editor or IDE.

Writing the Server Code

Next, let's write the code to create a basic HTTP server.

1. First, require the `http` module:

    ```
    const http = require('http');
    ```

2. Create a server that listens for incoming requests and sends a response:

    ```
    const server = http.createServer((req, res) => {
      // Set the response header to indicate a successful
    response
      res.writeHead(200, { 'Content-Type': 'text/plain' }
    );

      // Send the response body
      res.end('Hello, World!\n');
    });
    ```

3. Define the port on which the server will listen. By convention, let's use port 3000:

    ```
    const PORT = 3000;
    ```

4. Start the server and make it listen on the defined port:

    ```
    server.listen(PORT, () => {
      console.log(`Server is listening on port ${PORT}`);
    });
    ```

Complete Code Snippet

Here is the complete code for your `server.js` file:

```javascript
const http = require('http');

const server = http.createServer((req, res) => {
  res.writeHead(200, { 'Content-Type': 'text/plain' });
  res.end('Hello, World!\n');
});

const PORT = 3000;

server.listen(PORT, () => {
  console.log(`Server is listening on port ${PORT}`);
});
```

Running the Server

With your server code written, you can now run it:

1. In your terminal or command prompt, navigate to your project directory.

2. Run the following command to start the server:

   ```
   node server.js
   ```

Testing the Server

To ensure your server is running correctly, open a web browser and navigate to `http://localhost:3000`. You should see the message "Hello, World!" displayed in the browser.

Alternatively, you can use a tool like `curl` to test your server in the terminal:

```
curl http://localhost:3000
```

This command should return the following response:

```
Hello, World!
```

Summary

In this section, you have learned how to initialize a Node.js project, write a basic server using the `http` module, and test your server. These foundational skills are essential as we move forward and explore more advanced topics in building RESTful APIs with Node.js.

In the next subchapter, we will discuss how to configure routes to handle different types of HTTP requests.

5.3 Configuring Routes

In the previous subchapters, we set up our development environment and wrote a basic Node.js server. In this section, we will dive into configuring routes. Routing is a critical component of any server. It allows us to define how our server responds to different HTTP requests. Here, we'll learn how to configure routes in Node.js using code examples to help you understand the process.

Understanding Routes

A route is a section of Express code that associates an HTTP verb (GET, POST, PUT, DELETE, etc.) with a URL path and a function that handles the request. For example, a GET request to the URL `http://localhost:3000/sample-route` would be handled by a specific function in your server code.

Setting Up the Basics

First, let's ensure you have a basic Express.js server running. If you haven't set it up already, you can start by installing Express via npm:

```
npm install express
```

Next, create a new file called `server.js` and add the following basic implementation of an Express server:

```
const express = require('express');
const app = express();
const port = 3000;

app.listen(port, () => {
  console.log(`Server is running on http://localhost:${port}`);
});
```

Defining Routes

Let's configure some basic routes for our server. We'll start by handling a simple GET request. Add the following code to server.js:

```
app.get('/', (req, res) => {
  res.send('Hello, World!');
});
```

In this example, we have defined a route that listens for GET requests to the root URL (http://localhost:3000/). When a request is received at this URL, the server sends back a plain text response that says "Hello, World!".

Adding More Routes

You can define routes for other HTTP methods and paths using a similar pattern. Here are a few examples:

Handling a POST Request:

```
app.post('/submit', (req, res) => {
  res.send('POST request to /submit received');
});
```

In this case, the server responds to POST requests made to the URL http://localhost:3000/submit.

Handling a PUT Request:

```
app.put('/update', (req, res) => {
  res.send('PUT request to /update received');
});
```

Handling a DELETE Request:

```
app.delete('/delete', (req, res) => {
  res.send('DELETE request to /delete received');
});
```

Using Route Parameters

Route parameters allow you to capture values specified at certain positions in the URL. These values can be accessed through the req.params object. Here is an example:

```
app.get('/user/:id', (req, res) => {
  const userId = req.params.id;
  res.send(`User ID: ${userId}`);
});
```

With this route configuration, a GET request to http://localhost:3000/user/123 would capture the value 123 and respond with "User ID: 123".

Route Handlers with Middleware

You can also pass an array of middleware functions that process the request before sending a response.

```
const logMiddleware = (req, res, next) => {
  console.log(`Received request for ${req.url}`);
  next();
};

app.get('/info', logMiddleware, (req, res) => {
  res.send('Information Page');
});
```

In this example, `logMiddleware` logs the request URL to the console before passing control to the final route handler, which sends a response.

Summary

Configuring routes is an essential part of building a web server. By defining routes, you can control how your server responds to different types of HTTP requests. In this subchapter, we've covered basic route definitions using different HTTP methods, utilization of route parameters, and implementation of middleware functions within routes. These concepts will be foundational as we continue to build more complex functionalities and RESTful APIs in the later sections of this book.

5.4 Handling Requests and Responses

Handling requests and responses is a fundamental aspect of building a server with Node.js. It involves obtaining user input through HTTP requests, processing that input, and sending back relevant HTTP responses. This subchapter will guide you through the steps needed to retrieve data from client requests and send appropriate responses.

Understanding the Request Object

When a client makes a request to your server, Node.js provides an object representing that request. This request object contains several properties that allow you to access information such as the request URL, HTTP method, headers, and any body data.

Example: Accessing the Request URL

When a client makes a request, you can access the URL using the url property of the request object.

```javascript
const http = require('http');

const server = http.createServer((req, res) => {
  const url = req.url;
  console.log(`Request URL: ${url}`);
  // Additional code here
});

server.listen(3000, () => {
  console.log('Server is running at http://localhost:3000')
;
});
```

Example: Accessing the Request Method

You can also determine the HTTP method using the `method` property of the request object.

```javascript
const http = require('http');

const server = http.createServer((req, res) => {
  const method = req.method;
  console.log(`Request Method: ${method}`);
  // Additional code here
});

server.listen(3000, () => {
  console.log('Server is running at http://localhost:3000')
;
});
```

Example: Accessing Request Headers

To access request headers, you can use the `headers` property of the request object.

```javascript
const http = require('http');

const server = http.createServer((req, res) => {
  const headers = req.headers;
  console.log(`Request Headers: ${JSON.stringify(headers)}`
);
  // Additional code here
});

server.listen(3000, () => {
  console.log('Server is running at http://localhost:3000')
;
});
```

Understanding the Response Object

The response object is used to send data back to the client. This object provides methods to send headers, status codes, and the response body.

Example: Sending a Response

Here's a simple example of sending a plain text response.

```
const http = require('http');

const server = http.createServer((req, res) => {
  res.statusCode = 200;
  res.setHeader('Content-Type', 'text/plain');
  res.end('Hello, World!\n');
});

server.listen(3000, () => {
  console.log('Server is running at http://localhost:3000')
;
});
```

Setting HTTP Status Codes and Headers

You can set the HTTP status code using the statusCode property, and you can set response headers using the setHeader method.

```
const http = require('http');

const server = http.createServer((req, res) => {
  res.statusCode = 200;
  res.setHeader('Content-Type', 'application/json');
  res.end(JSON.stringify({ message: 'Hello, JSON!' }));
});

server.listen(3000, () => {
  console.log('Server is running at http://localhost:3000')
;
});
```

Handling JSON Data

Often, you'll be dealing with JSON data. Here's how to parse JSON data from a request and respond with JSON.

Example: Parsing JSON Data from the Request Body

You need to gather the data chunks and parse them.

```javascript
const http = require('http');

const server = http.createServer((req, res) => {
  if (req.method === 'POST') {
    let body = '';

    req.on('data', chunk => {
      body += chunk.toString();
    });

    req.on('end', () => {
      const data = JSON.parse(body);
      console.log(data);
      res.statusCode = 200;
      res.setHeader('Content-Type', 'application/json');
      res.end(JSON.stringify({ message: 'Data received', da
ta }));
    });
  } else {
    res.statusCode = 404;
    res.end();
  }
});

server.listen(3000, () => {
  console.log('Server is running at http://localhost:3000')
;
});
```

Handling Different Routes

You can handle different types of requests by examining the url and method properties together.

Example: Handling GET and POST Requests at Different Routes

```javascript
const http = require('http');

const server = http.createServer((req, res) => {
  if (req.url === '/' && req.method === 'GET') {
    res.statusCode = 200;
    res.setHeader('Content-Type', 'text/plain');
    res.end('Hello, GET!\n');
  } else if (req.url === '/data' && req.method === 'POST')
{
    let body = '';
    req.on('data', chunk => {
      body += chunk.toString();
    });
    req.on('end', () => {
      const data = JSON.parse(body);
      res.statusCode = 200;
      res.setHeader('Content-Type', 'application/json');
      res.end(JSON.stringify({ message: 'Hello, POST!', dat
a }));
    });
  } else {
    res.statusCode = 404;
    res.setHeader('Content-Type', 'text/plain');
    res.end('Not Found\n');
  }
});

server.listen(3000, () => {
  console.log('Server is running at http://localhost:3000')
;
});
```

By understanding and utilizing the request and response objects, you can create a Node.js server that effectively handles different types of client interactions. This forms the basis for building more complex RESTful APIs, which you will explore in the upcoming chapters.

6. Working with Express.js

6.1. Introduction to Express.js

Express.js is a popular web framework for Node.js that simplifies the process of building robust and scalable web applications and APIs. By providing a thin layer of fundamental web application features, it enables developers to create server-side applications with ease. In this subchapter, we will explore the key features of Express.js, its advantages, and provide an overview of how it integrates with Node.js to develop RESTful APIs.

What is Express.js?

Express.js is a minimal and flexible Node.js web application framework that provides a rich set of features for building web and mobile applications. It is heavily inspired by the Ruby on Rails and Sinatra frameworks, but it is designed to work specifically within the Node.js environment. This synergy provides an efficient and non-blocking I/O model, making it highly performant and suitable for real-time applications.

Key Features of Express.js

- **Minimalistic**: Express.js offers a minimalistic approach, with only the essential features to start. You can add additional modules and middleware as needed.

- **Middleware**: Middleware functions in Express.js provide powerful mechanisms to handle HTTP requests in a modular and reusable way.

- **Routing**: Express.js brings an intuitive and flexible routing mechanism for handling various HTTP methods and URL patterns.

- **Templating**: The framework allows integration with several templating engines to generate dynamic HTML content.

- **RESTful APIs**: Developing RESTful services with Express.js is straightforward, with support for various content types and methods.

- **Extensibility**: It is easy to extend Express.js with numerous community-driven middleware and modules available via npm.

Advantages of Using Express.js

- **Rapid Development**: Its minimalistic core and middleware capabilities speed up the development process.

- **Scalability**: Express.js applications are scalable, handling numerous simultaneous connections with high efficiency.

- **Community Support**: With a large and active community, there is ample support, a wealth of plugins, and extensive documentation.

- **Flexibility**: Developers have the freedom to structure their applications and incorporate a wide range of functionalities as per requirements.

- **Compatibility**: Being a part of the Node.js ecosystem, Express.js seamlessly integrates with other JavaScript libraries and tools.

Hello World Example

Let's dive into a simple "Hello World" example to see how straightforward it is to get started with Express.js.

First, you need to initialize your Node.js project and install Express.js:

```
npm init -y
npm install express
```

Create a file named `app.js` and write the following code:

```
const express = require('express');
const app = express();

app.get('/', (req, res) => {
  res.send('Hello World!');
});

const PORT = process.env.PORT || 3000;
app.listen(PORT, () => {
  console.log(`Server is running on http://localhost:${PORT
}`);
});
```

To run the application, execute:

```
node app.js
```

Visit `http://localhost:3000` in your browser, and you should see the message "Hello World!".

Understanding the Basic Code

- **Import Express**: We start by requiring the Express module.
- **Initialize the App**: An instance of an Express application is created.
- **Define a Route**: We define a basic route that responds with "Hello World!" when a GET request is made to the root URL.
- **Start the Server**: The app listens on port 3000 (or a port specified in the environment variables), and logs a message once the server is running.

Integrating with Node.js

Express.js leverages Node.js's asynchronous I/O and event-driven architecture, enabling the creation of high-performance web applications. It's particularly useful for applications that require real-time communication, such as chat apps or live updates.

By utilizing Express.js, developers can focus on writing application logic without worrying about the low-level details of HTTP server management, making it an indispensable tool in modern Node.js development.

In the following sections, we will delve deeper into setting up Express.js, building routes, and effectively using middleware to enhance our applications.

6.2. Setting Up Express.js

Setting up Express.js is the first step towards building a robust RESTful API with Node.js. Express.js is a minimalist web framework for Node.js, providing a wide range of features for building web and mobile applications. In this section, we will walk through the steps to set up Express.js and create a basic server.

Installing Express.js

Before installing Express.js, ensure you have Node.js and npm (Node Package Manager) installed on your machine. First, navigate to your project directory and initialize a new Node.js project using the following command:

```
npm init -y
```

The -y flag automatically answers 'yes' to all prompts, generating a package.json file with default values.

Next, install Express.js by running:

```
npm install express --save
```

This command installs Express.js and adds it as a dependency in your package.json file.

Creating a Basic Express Server

To create a basic server using Express.js, follow these steps:

1. **Create an Entry File**: Typically, the entry file for a Node.js application is named index.js or app.js. Create a file named index.js in your project root.

2. **Import Express Module**: Require the Express.js module in your index.js file.

3. **Initialize Express App**: Create an instance of an Express app.

4. **Define a Route**: Set up a simple route to test the server.

5. **Start the Server**: Instruct the app to listen on a specified port.

Here is an example of these steps in code:

```
// Import the Express.js module
const express = require('express');

// Initialize an instance of Express
const app = express();

// Define a simple route
app.get('/', (req, res) => {
  res.send('Hello, world!');
});

// Start the server and listen on port 3000
const PORT = 3000;
app.listen(PORT, () => {
  console.log(`Server is running at http://localhost:${PORT
}`);
});
```

Testing the Server

To test the server, run the following command in your terminal:

```
node index.js
```

You should see output indicating that the server is running:

```
Server is running at http://localhost:3000
```

Open your web browser and navigate to http://localhost:3000. You should see the message "Hello, world!" displayed.

Handling Different Routes

Express.js allows you to define various routes to handle different HTTP methods such as GET, POST, PUT, and DELETE. Here's an example of how to set up a route to handle POST requests:

```
// Define a route to handle POST requests
app.post('/submit', (req, res) => {
  res.send('POST request to the /submit endpoint');
});
```

Similarly, you can define routes for PUT and DELETE methods:

```
// Define a route to handle PUT requests
app.put('/update', (req, res) => {
  res.send('PUT request to the /update endpoint');
});

// Define a route to handle DELETE requests
app.delete('/delete', (req, res) => {
  res.send('DELETE request to the /delete endpoint');
});
```

Using Middleware

Middleware functions are functions that have access to the request object (req), the response object (res), and the next middleware function in the application's request-response cycle. In the next subchapter, we will dive deeper into using middleware in Express.js. For now, here is a simple example of middleware in action:

```
// A simple middleware function
app.use((req, res, next) => {
  console.log('A request was made to: ' + req.url);
  next(); // Pass control to the next handler
});
```

This middleware function logs the requested URL to the console each time a request is made to the server.

By following these steps, you will have a basic Express.js server up and running. This foundational knowledge will allow you to build more complex and feature-rich applications as we progress through the book. In the next section, we will explore how to build and manage routes more efficiently.

6.3. Building Basic Routes

In this section, we'll delve into one of the core features of Express.js – routing. Routing refers to determining how an application's endpoints (URIs) respond to client requests. In this part of the book, we will learn to create simple routes to handle HTTP requests.

Understanding Routes

In Express.js, routes are defined using methods corresponding to HTTP verbs. The most common HTTP verbs are:

- GET: To retrieve data.
- POST: To submit data.
- PUT: To update data.
- DELETE: To delete data.

Each routing method requires a URL path and a callback function that knows what to do when the endpoint is hit.

Setting Up Basic Routes

Before we start building routes, ensure you have set up your Express.js environment as described in the previous sections. Now, let's create a basic Express.js application with simple routes.

Creating a Basic Express Application

First, create a new file named app.js if it doesn't already exist. Initialize your project, set up Express, and then proceed to define your routes.

```
const express = require('express');
const app = express();
const port = 3000;

app.listen(port, () => {
  console.log(`Server is running on http://localhost:${port
}`);
});
```

Adding a Basic GET Route

A GET route retrieves data from the server. Let's create a basic route that returns a welcome message when accessed.

```
app.get('/', (req, res) => {
  res.send('Welcome to our Express.js application!');
});
```

When you navigate to `http://localhost:3000/` in your browser, you should see the message: "Welcome to our Express.js application!".

Defining a POST Route

A POST route is typically used for submitting data to the server. Create a route that listens for POST requests and responds with a confirmation message.

```
app.use(express.json());

app.post('/submit', (req, res) => {
  const data = req.body;
  res.send(`Data received: ${JSON.stringify(data)}`);
});
```

To test this, you would need to send a POST request to `http://localhost:3000/submit` with some JSON data.

Implementing a PUT Route

A PUT route is used to update existing data. Here's how you can define a PUT route in your application.

```
app.put('/update', (req, res) => {
  const updateData = req.body;
  res.send(`Data updated: ${JSON.stringify(updateData)}`);
});
```

Access this route by making a PUT request to `http://localhost:3000/update` with some JSON data in the request body.

Creating a DELETE Route

A DELETE route is used for deleting data. Let's see how you can define a simple DELETE route.

```
app.delete('/delete/:id', (req, res) => {
  const id = req.params.id;
  res.send(`Data with ID ${id} has been deleted`);
});
```

This route listens for DELETE requests at `http://localhost:3000/delete/:id`, where `:id` is a parameter that lets you specify which record you want to delete.

Summary

In this section, we learned how to build basic routes using Express.js. This forms the foundation of any Express.js application as it determines how the application responds to different HTTP requests. As you move forward, you'll learn to build more complex routes and handle various types of middleware, making your application robust and more functional.

6.4. Middleware Functions and Usage

Middleware functions are a fundamental part of an Express.js application. These functions have access to the request object (req), the response object (res), and the next middleware function in the application's request-response cycle. Middleware can execute any code, make changes to the request and response objects, end the request-response cycle, or call the next middleware function in the stack.

Understanding Middleware

A middleware function is essentially a function that takes three parameters: req, res, and next. The core concept of middleware is to perform sequential processing of the request and response objects, allowing for operations such as request logging, authentication, and error handling.

Here's a simple example of a middleware function that logs the request method and URL:

```
const express = require('express');
const app = express();

const requestLogger = (req, res, next) => {
  console.log(`${req.method} ${req.url}`);
  next(); // Pass control to the next middleware function
};

app.use(requestLogger);

app.get('/example', (req, res) => {
  res.send('Middleware example!');
});

app.listen(3000, () => {
  console.log('Server is running on port 3000');
});
```

Types of Middleware

Middleware can be classified into several types based on their functionality and usage within an Express.js application:

Application-level Middleware

Application-level middleware are bound to an instance of the express object using app.use() or app.METHOD(). They are functions that are executed for every request that matches the routes they're defined in.

```
const app = express();

app.use((req, res, next) => {
  console.log('Application-level middleware');
  next();
});

app.get('/app-level', (req, res) => {
  res.send('Application-level middleware example');
});
```

Router-level Middleware

Router-level middleware works in the same way as application-level middleware but is bound to an instance of express.Router().

```
const router = express.Router();

router.use((req, res, next) => {
  console.log('Router-level middleware');
  next();
});

router.get('/router-level', (req, res) => {
  res.send('Router-level middleware example');
});

app.use('/api', router);
```

Error-handling Middleware

Error-handling middleware functions have four arguments instead of three: err, req, res, and next. Such functions are used to handle errors occurring in the application.

```
app.use((err, req, res, next) => {
  console.error(err.stack);
  res.status(500).send('Something broke!');
});
```

Built-in Middleware

Express also provides built-in middleware functions for common tasks like serving static files and parsing request bodies.

Serving Static Files

You can serve static files (e.g., images, CSS files, JavaScript files) using the express.static middleware function.

```
app.use(express.static('public'));
```

Accessing http://localhost:3000/images/logo.png will serve the logo.png file from the public/images directory.

Body Parsing

Body-parsing middleware is used to parse the body section of incoming request streams and make it accessible under req.body.

```
app.use(express.json());
app.use(express.urlencoded({ extended: true }));

app.post('/data', (req, res) => {
  console.log(req.body);
  res.send('Body parsed!');
});
```

Using Third-Party Middleware

In addition to custom and built-in middleware, you can use middleware developed by the community. For example, `morgan` is a popular middleware for logging HTTP requests.

```
const morgan = require('morgan');
app.use(morgan('tiny'));
```

Chaining Middleware

Multiple middleware functions can be chained together by calling `next()` in each function.

```
const middlewareOne = (req, res, next) => {
  console.log('Middleware One');
  next();
};

const middlewareTwo = (req, res, next) => {
  console.log('Middleware Two');
  next();
};

app.use(middlewareOne, middlewareTwo);

app.get('/chain', (req, res) => {
  res.send('Chained middleware example');
});
```

Conclusion

Middleware functions are pivotal in building robust and maintainable Express.js applications. By understanding their usage and capabilities, you can effectively handle tasks like logging, parsing, authentication, error handling, and more, leading to a more organized and efficient codebase.

7. Middleware Functions

7.1 Introduction to Middleware Functions

Middleware functions are a core concept in building scalable and maintainable RESTful APIs with Node.js, particularly when using the Express.js framework. Middleware, in the context of Express, is a function that has access to the request object (req), the response object (res), and the next function in the application's request-response cycle. Middleware functions can perform tasks ranging from parsing request bodies to handling errors, making them indispensable in a well-architected Express application.

What is Middleware?

Middleware functions are functions that execute in the middle of the request-response cycle. They have a broad array of applications:

- Executing any code.
- Making changes to the request and response objects.
- Concluding the request-response cycle.
- Calling the next middleware function in the stack.

Basic Structure of Middleware

A middleware function typically follows this structure:

```
function middlewareFunction(req, res, next) {
  // Perform some operations
  next(); // Pass control to the next middleware function
}
```

It's crucial to call the next() function; otherwise, the request will be left hanging. If next() is not called or if the response is not ended, the request will not proceed to the next middleware function or route handler.

Using Middleware in Express

In Express applications, middleware functions can be used either globally or on a per-route basis.

Global Middleware

Global middleware functions run for every incoming request. You can apply these middleware functions using the app.use() method:

```
const express = require('express');
const app = express();

function globalMiddleware(req, res, next) {
  console.log(`Request URL: ${req.url}`);
  next();
}

app.use(globalMiddleware);

app.get('http://example.com/', (req, res) => {
  res.send('Home Page');
});

app.listen(3000, () => {
  console.log('Server is running on port 3000');
});
```

In this example, globalMiddleware is applied to all routes. It logs the request URL and then calls next() to pass control to the next middleware function or route handler.

Route-specific Middleware

Middleware functions can also be applied to individual routes:

```javascript
const express = require('express');
const app = express();

function routeMiddleware(req, res, next) {
  console.log('Route-specific Middleware');
  next();
}

app.get('http://example.com/user', routeMiddleware, (req, r
es) => {
  res.send('User Page');
});

app.listen(3000, () => {
  console.log('Server is running on port 3000');
});
```

Here, `routeMiddleware` only applies to the `/user` route.

Common Use Cases for Middleware

Middleware functions can be used for a variety of tasks in an Express application:

Logging

You can create middleware functions to log details about each request:

```javascript
function logger(req, res, next) {
  console.log(`${req.method} ${req.url}`);
  next();
}

app.use(logger);
```

Authentication

Authentication middleware can be used to protect routes:

```javascript
function authenticate(req, res, next) {
  if (req.headers['authorization']) {
    next();
  } else {
    res.status(401).send('Unauthorized');
  }
}

app.get('http://example.com/protected', authenticate, (req,
res) => {
  res.send('Protected Page');
});
```

Error Handling

Middleware functions can also handle errors:

```javascript
function errorHandler(err, req, res, next) {
  console.error(err.stack);
  res.status(500).send('Something broke!');
}

app.use(errorHandler);
```

Conclusion

Middleware functions are powerful tools that facilitate modular and maintainable code in Express applications. They provide a flexible way to handle a variety of tasks, from logging and authentication to error handling. As you continue your journey through this book, you'll find that understanding and effectively utilizing middleware is crucial for building robust RESTful APIs with Node.js and Express. In the next sections, we will delve deeper into creating custom middleware, utilizing third-party middleware, and error handling middleware functions.

7.2 Creating Custom Middleware

Middleware functions in Express.js are functions that have access to the request object (req), the response object (res), and the next middleware function in the application's request-response cycle. They can execute any code, make changes to the req and res objects, end the request-response cycle, and call the next middleware function in the stack.

In this subchapter, we will delve into creating custom middleware functions and integrating them into your Express.js application. Custom middleware can be used for a variety of purposes including logging, authentication, and modifying the request or response objects.

Creating a Simple Logging Middleware

Creating middleware in Express.js is straightforward. Let's start with a simple logging middleware that logs request details to the console:

```
const express = require('express');
const app = express();

// Logging Middleware
function logRequest(req, res, next) {
  console.log(`${req.method} ${req.url}`);
  next();   // Pass control to the next middleware
}

app.use(logRequest);

app.get('http://localhost:3000', (req, res) => {
  res.send('Hello World');
});

app.listen(3000, () => {
  console.log('Server is running on http://localhost:3000')
;
});
```

In this example, the logRequest middleware function logs the HTTP method and URL of each request. The next() function indicates that the middleware is done and the next middleware function should be executed.

Adding Authorization Middleware

Next, let's create an authorization middleware that only allows requests with a specific header to proceed:

```
// Authorization Middleware
function authorize(req, res, next) {
  const token = req.headers['authorization'];

  if (token === 'secret-token') {
    next(); // Authorized, proceed to the next middleware
  } else {
    res.status(403).send('Forbidden');
  }
}

app.use(authorize);

app.get('http://localhost:3000/protected', (req, res) => {
  res.send('Protected Resource');
});
```

This middleware checks if the authorization header equals 'secret-token'. If the token is correct, it calls next() to proceed. Otherwise, it responds with a 403 Forbidden status.

Middleware for Parsing JSON

Middleware can also be used to parse request bodies. Although Express provides built-in middleware like express.json(), you can create your own. Below is an example:

```
const bodyParser = (req, res, next) => {
  let data = '';

  req.on('data', chunk => {
    data += chunk;
  });

  req.on('end', () => {
    try {
      req.body = JSON.parse(data);
    } catch (e) {
      req.body = {};
    }
    next();
  });
};

app.use(bodyParser);

app.post('http://localhost:3000/data', (req, res) => {
  res.send(`Received data: ${JSON.stringify(req.body)}`);
});
```

Here, the bodyParser middleware function assembles the data chunks, parses them as JSON, and attaches the result to req.body before calling next().

Combining Multiple Middleware Functions

Middleware functions can be combined to create a modular and reusable code. For example, you can combine the logging and authorization middleware:

```
app.use(logRequest);
app.use(authorize);

app.get('http://localhost:3000/secure', (req, res) => {
  res.send('This is a secure endpoint');
});
```

In this setup, `logRequest` runs first, followed by `authorize`. If the request passes both middleware checks, the route handler executes.

Conclusion

Custom middleware functions are powerful tools that can help you manage and preprocess requests in your Express.js applications. By understanding how to create and use these functions, you can enhance the functionality, security, and maintainability of your APIs. In the next section, we will explore using third-party middleware to further extend your application's capabilities.

7.3 Using Third-party Middleware

In addition to creating custom middleware, Express.js allows you to leverage a variety of powerful third-party middleware to extend the functionality of your application. These middleware functions are maintained by the community and come with robust features that can save you a lot of time and effort. This section will guide you through some common third-party middleware packages, demonstrate their usage, and show how they can be integrated into your RESTful API built with Node.js.

Body Parsing with body-parser

One of the commonly used middleware libraries is body-parser. This middleware parses incoming request bodies in a middleware before your handlers, available under the req.body property. It supports various content types, including JSON, urlencoded, and raw.

To use body-parser, first install it via npm:

```
npm install body-parser
```

Then, include and configure it in your Express application:

```
const express = require('express');
const bodyParser = require('body-parser');

const app = express();

// Parse application/json
app.use(bodyParser.json());

// Parse application/x-www-form-urlencoded
app.use(bodyParser.urlencoded({ extended: true }));

app.post('http://{your_domain_or_ip}/data', (req, res) => {
    res.send(`Received data: ${JSON.stringify(req.body)}`);
});

app.listen(3000, () => {
    console.log('Server is running on port 3000');
});
```

CORS with `cors`

Cross-Origin Resource Sharing (CORS) is a mechanism that allows restricted resources on a web page to be requested from another domain. To allow CORS in your application, you can use the `cors` middleware.

First, install the `cors` package:

```
npm install cors
```

Then, integrate it into your application:

```
const express = require('express');
const cors = require('cors');

const app = express();

// Enable All CORS Requests
app.use(cors());

app.get('http://{your_domain_or_ip}/resource', (req, res) =
> {
    res.send('This resource is CORS-enabled');
});

app.listen(3000, () => {
    console.log('Server is running on port 3000');
});
```

If you need more control over the CORS configuration, you can pass options to the cors middleware:

```
app.use(cors({ origin: 'http://{specific_domain_or_ip}' }))
;
```

Logging with morgan

Logging requests and responses can be vital for debugging and monitoring your application. The morgan middleware simplifies request logging.

Install morgan via npm:

```
npm install morgan
```

Then, use morgan in your application:

```
const express = require('express');
const morgan = require('morgan');

const app = express();

// Use morgan to log requests to the console
app.use(morgan('combined'));

app.get('http://{your_domain_or_ip}/', (req, res) => {
    res.send('Logging with morgan');
});

app.listen(3000, () => {
    console.log('Server is running on port 3000');
});
```

Cookie Handling with `cookie-parser`

Cookies are often used for storing user session data in a web application. The `cookie-parser` middleware parses cookie header and populates `req.cookies` with an object keyed by the cookie names.

Install `cookie-parser`:

```
npm install cookie-parser
```

Then configure it as middleware:

```
const express = require('express');
const cookieParser = require('cookie-parser');

const app = express();

// Use cookie-parser middleware
app.use(cookieParser());

app.get('http://{your_domain_or_ip}/', (req, res) => {
    // Set a cookie
    res.cookie('token', '123456789');
    res.send('Cookie has been set');
});

app.get('http://{your_domain_or_ip}/cookies', (req, res) =>
{
    // Retrieve cookies
    res.send(req.cookies);
});

app.listen(3000, () => {
    console.log('Server is running on port 3000');
});
```

Security with `helmet`

Security is crucial for any application exposed to the internet. `helmet` is a middleware package that helps secure Express apps by setting various HTTP headers.

Install `helmet`:

```
npm install helmet
```

Use it in your application:

```
const express = require('express');
const helmet = require('helmet');

const app = express();

// Use helmet to secure the app
app.use(helmet());

app.get('http://{your_domain_or_ip}/', (req, res) => {
    res.send('Helmet is securing this app');
});

app.listen(3000, () => {
    console.log('Server is running on port 3000');
});
```

Rate Limiting with `express-rate-limit`

Rate limiting is essential to protect your application from brute-force attacks and abuse. `express-rate-limit` is a middleware for rate-limiting incoming requests.

Install `express-rate-limit`:

```
npm install express-rate-limit
```

Then set it up:

```javascript
const express = require('express');
const rateLimit = require('express-rate-limit');

const app = express();

// Apply rate limiting to all requests
const limiter = rateLimit({
    windowMs: 15 * 60 * 1000, // 15 minutes
    max: 100, // Limit each IP to 100 requests per window (
15 mins)
});

app.use(limiter);

app.get('http://{your_domain_or_ip}/', (req, res) => {
    res.send('Rate limiting is in effect');
});

app.listen(3000, () => {
    console.log('Server is running on port 3000');
});
```

By leveraging these third-party middleware solutions, you can enhance the functionality, security, and maintainability of your RESTful APIs built with Node.js. Always ensure you understand the middleware functions and how they impact your application to avoid performance bottlenecks and security risks.

7.4 Error Handling Middleware Functions

Error handling is a vital part of building robust APIs. Proper error handling ensures that your application provides meaningful responses to clients while also maintaining the integrity of your server. In Express.js, handling errors is made easier through the use of specialized middleware functions. In this subchapter, we will cover how to create error handling middleware, utilize them effectively, and integrate them into your Express application.

Understanding Error Handling Middleware

Error handling middleware in Express.js is defined with four parameters: `err`, `req`, `res`, and `next`. The `err` parameter is used to capture any errors that occur during the request-response cycle. This type of middleware is invoked whenever an error is passed to the `next()` function, allowing you to create custom logic for handling errors.

```javascript
function errorHandler(err, req, res, next) {
    console.error(err.stack);
    res.status(500).json({ message: 'An internal server err
or occurred.' });
}

// Integrate the error handler middleware into your Express
application
const express = require('express');
const app = express();

// Example route
app.get('/api/error', (req, res) => {
    throw new Error('Something went wrong!');
});

// Use the error handler middleware
app.use(errorHandler);

// Start the server
const PORT = 3000;
app.listen(PORT, () => {
    console.log(`Server is running on http://localhost:${PO
RT}`);
});
```

Creating Custom Error Handlers

Custom error handlers allow you to tailor responses based on the type of error that occurs. You can create different error handling middleware for different types of errors to improve the clarity and usefulness of your error responses.

```
function notFoundHandler(req, res, next) {
    res.status(404).json({ message: 'Resource not found.' }
);
}

// General error handler for other types of errors
function generalErrorHandler(err, req, res, next) {
    if (res.headersSent) {
        return next(err);
    }
    res.status(500).json({ message: 'An internal server err
or occurred.' });
}

// Set up the Express application
const express = require('express');
const app = express();

// Example route
app.get('/api/resource', (req, res) => {
    res.send('Resource found!');
});

// Middleware to simulate a route not found scenario
app.use((req, res, next) => {
    next();
});

// Use custom error handlers
app.use(notFoundHandler);
app.use(generalErrorHandler);

// Start the server
const PORT = 3000;
app.listen(PORT, () => {
    console.log(`Server is running on http://localhost:${PO
RT}`);
});
```

Handling Specific Errors

You can create error handling middleware that handles specific types of errors. This is especially useful when dealing with different error statuses like `400 Bad Request`, `401 Unauthorized`, or `500 Internal Server Error`.

```
class ClientError extends Error {
    constructor(message, status = 400) {
        super(message);
        this.status = status;
    }
}

// Middleware for handling client errors
function clientErrorHandler(err, req, res, next) {
    if (err instanceof ClientError) {
        res.status(err.status).json({ message: err.message
});
    } else {
        next(err); // Passes the error to the next middlewa
re
    }
}

// General error handler for other types of errors
function generalErrorHandler(err, req, res, next) {
    res.status(500).json({ message: 'An internal server err
or occurred.' });
}

// Set up the Express application
const express = require('express');
const app = express();

// Example route with a client error
app.get('/api/client-error', (req, res, next) => {
    next(new ClientError('Invalid client input', 400));
});

// Use error handlers
app.use(clientErrorHandler);
app.use(generalErrorHandler);

// Start the server
const PORT = 3000;
app.listen(PORT, () => {
    console.log(`Server is running on http://localhost:${PO
RT}`);
});
```

Remember to Order Your Middleware Correctly

The order in which middleware functions are declared in your application matters. Ensure that your error handling middleware is listed after your other middleware and routes. Express will use them in the order they are declared, so placing error handlers at the end ensures that they are called only after other middleware and routes have been tried and have either succeeded or failed.

Conclusion

Error handling middleware is an essential part of building reliable and maintainable RESTful APIs with Node.js and Express.js. By carefully creating and using error handling middleware, you can provide meaningful and helpful error responses to your API clients, thereby improving the overall robustness and user experience of your application.

8. Routing in Express

8.1 Routing Basics

Routing in Express is a fundamental concept that allows you to define how your application responds to various HTTP requests end-points. Efficient routing is crucial in building robust and maintainable RESTful APIs. In this section, we will cover the basics of routing, from setting up routes to handling different types of requests.

What is Routing?

Routing refers to how an application's endpoints (URIs) respond to client requests. In Express, a router is essentially a middleware that manages different paths and HTTP methods to determine the correct response for a request.

Setting Up Basic Routes

Setting up routes in Express is straightforward. You create routes by specifying the HTTP method (GET, POST, etc.) and the path. Let's start by setting up a few basic routes.

Example: Setting up a simple Express application

```
const express = require('express');
const app = express();

// Basic GET route
app.get('/', (req, res) => {
  res.send('Welcome to the Homepage!');
});

// Another GET route
app.get('/about', (req, res) => {
  res.send('This is the About page.');
});

// Start the server
const PORT = process.env.PORT || 3000;
app.listen(PORT, () => {
  console.log(`Server is running on port ${PORT}`);
});
```

In this example: - `app.get('/', ...)` handles GET requests to the root URL (`http://localhost:3000/`). - `app.get('/about', ...)` handles GET requests to the "About" page (`http://localhost:3000/about`).

Path Parameters

You can extend your routes to handle dynamic segments of the URL, known as route parameters. These parameters are specified by placing a colon (`:`) before the variable name in the route path.

Example: Handling path parameters

```
// GET route with a parameter
app.get('/user/:userId', (req, res) => {
  res.send(`User ID: ${req.params.userId}`);
});
```

Here, accessing `http://localhost:3000/user/123` will output `User ID: 123`.

Query Parameters

Query parameters allow you to pass data to the server via the URL in a key-value pair format. These parameters are appended to the URL after a question mark (?).

Example: Handling query parameters

```
// GET route with query parameters
app.get('/search', (req, res) => {
  const { term, page } = req.query;
  res.send(`Search Term: ${term}, Page: ${page}`);
});
```

Visiting http://localhost:3000/search?term=nodejs&page=2 will output Search Term: nodejs, Page: 2.

Organizing Routes

For a more organized codebase, you might prefer to separate your route definitions into different files. Express provides the express.Router class to help with this.

Example: Creating a Router module

First, create a new file routes.js.

```
// routes.js
const express = require('express');
const router = express.Router();

// Define routes here
router.get('/', (req, res) => {
  res.send('Welcome to the Homepage from Router!');
});

router.get('/about', (req, res) => {
  res.send('This is the About page from Router.');
});

module.exports = router;
```

Then, include this router in your main application file.

```
// app.js
const express = require('express');
const app = express();
const routes = require('./routes');

// Use the routes from the router module
app.use('/', routes);

const PORT = process.env.PORT || 3000;
app.listen(PORT, () => {
  console.log(`Server is running on port ${PORT}`);
});
```

In this setup: - The `routes` module defines the routing logic. - The main application uses the routes via `app.use('/', routes);`.

Summary

In this section, we have explored the basics of routing in Express. We learned how to set up simple routes, handle path and query parameters, and organize routes using the `express.Router` class. Understanding these routing fundamentals will serve as a strong foundation for creating more complex and efficient API endpoints.

8.2 Route Parameters

Route parameters in Express.js are a crucial feature allowing developers to capture values from the URL and use them in the route handling logic. This feature is especially useful when building RESTful APIs wherein resources are often manipulated using their unique identifiers.

What are Route Parameters?

Route parameters are placeholders in the URL that are prefixed by a colon (:). These placeholders can be used to capture values from the URL and make them accessible within the route handler. For example, consider the route definition /users/:userId. The :userId is a route parameter that can capture different user IDs from the URL.

Defining Route Parameters

The basic syntax for defining a route with parameters in Express.js is as follows:

```
app.get('/users/:userId', (req, res) => {
    const userId = req.params.userId;
    res.send(`User ID: ${userId}`);
});
```

In this example, the route definition /users/:userId will match any URL that starts with /users/ followed by any value (e.g., /users/123, /users/abc).

Accessing Route Parameters

Route parameters can be accessed using the `req.params` object, where each parameter is a key-value pair. Here is an example of a route handling logic that fetches a user based on the user ID:

```
app.get('/users/:userId', (req, res) => {
    const userId = req.params.userId;

    // Simulate fetching user from a database
    const user = {
        id: userId,
        name: "John Doe"
    };

    res.json(user);
});
```

Using Multiple Parameters

Express.js allows defining multiple route parameters in a single URL path. For instance, you can define a route with both `userId` and `postId` parameters:

```
app.get('/users/:userId/posts/:postId', (req, res) => {
    const userId = req.params.userId;
    const postId = req.params.postId;

    res.send(`User ID: ${userId}, Post ID: ${postId}`);
});
```

Given the above route, both `/users/1/posts/10` and `/users/2/posts/20` will be valid URLs that the server can handle.

Optional Parameters

Route parameters can also be optional by appending a ? after the parameter name. Here is an example:

```
app.get('/users/:userId/posts/:postId?', (req, res) => {
    const userId = req.params.userId;
    const postId = req.params.postId;

    if (postId) {
        res.send(`User ID: ${userId}, Post ID: ${postId}`);
    } else {
        res.send(`User ID: ${userId}`);
    }
});
```

In this case, the route will handle both /users/1/posts/10 and /users/1.

Using Regular Expressions

Express.js supports the use of regular expressions to define more complex routing patterns. This can be useful for imposing constraints on the route parameters. For example, to match user IDs that are only numeric, you can use:

```
app.get('/users/:userId(\\d+)', (req, res) => {
    const userId = req.params.userId;
    res.send(`User ID: ${userId}`);
});
```

The route /users/:userId(\\d+) will match /users/123 but not /users/abc.

Practical Example

To demonstrate a practical example, consider an API endpoint that fetches details of a specific book from a library by its ID:

```
app.get('/library/books/:bookId', (req, res) => {
    const bookId = req.params.bookId;

    // Mock book data for demonstration
    const books = [
        { id: '1', title: '1984', author: 'George Orwell' }
,
        { id: '2', title: 'To Kill a Mockingbird', author:
'Harper Lee' },
    ];

    const book = books.find(b => b.id === bookId);

    if (book) {
        res.json(book);
    } else {
        res.status(404).send('Book not found');
    }
});
```

In this example, the route /library/books/:bookId captures the book ID from the URL and uses it to find the corresponding book details in the array. If the book is found, it returns the book data as a JSON response; otherwise, it sends a 404 status code indicating the book is not found.

Route parameters provide a flexible and powerful way to capture and utilize dynamic values from the URL, making it easier to build RESTful endpoints that are both functional and efficient.

8.3 Handling Different HTTP Methods

When building RESTful APIs with Express.js, understanding and handling different HTTP methods is critical. Each HTTP method corresponds to a different operation and is used to represent actions on server resources. This subchapter will focus on how to handle these methods effectively when setting up your routes in Express.

HTTP Methods Overview

The primary HTTP methods you'll work with in RESTful APIs are:

- GET: Retrieve data from the server.
- POST: Send data to the server to create a new resource.
- PUT: Send data to the server to update an existing resource.
- DELETE: Remove a resource from the server.

Handling GET Requests

A GET request is used to fetch data. In Express, you handle GET requests using the .get() method.

```
const express = require('express');
const app = express();

app.get('/api/users', (req, res) => {
  // Assume we fetch users from a database
  const users = [
    { id: 1, name: 'John Doe' },
    { id: 2, name: 'Jane Smith' }
  ];
  res.json(users);
});

app.listen(3000, () => {
  console.log('Server is running on http://localhost:3000')
;
});
```

When a GET request is made to `http://localhost:3000/api/users`, the server responds with a JSON array of user objects.

Handling POST Requests

A POST request sends data to the server to create a new resource. Use the `.post()` method in Express to handle POST requests.

```
app.post('/api/users', (req, res) => {
  const newUser = {
    id: Date.now(), // Generate a unique ID
    name: req.body.name
  };
  // Here you would normally insert into the database
  res.status(201).json(newUser);
});
```

To make a POST request to `http://localhost:3000/api/users`, include the user data in the request body. The server responds with the newly created user object, and a `201 Created` status.

Handling PUT Requests

A PUT request updates an existing resource. Use the `.put()` method in Express to handle PUT requests.

```
app.put('/api/users/:id', (req, res) => {
  const userId = req.params.id;
  const updatedUser = {
    id: userId,
    name: req.body.name
  };
  // Normally you would update the user in the database here

  res.json(updatedUser);
});
```

When a PUT request is made to `http://localhost:3000/api/users/:id`, include the updated user data in the request body. The server responds with the updated user object.

Handling DELETE Requests

A DELETE request removes a resource from the server. Use the `.delete()` method in Express to handle DELETE requests.

```
app.delete('/api/users/:id', (req, res) => {
  const userId = req.params.id;
  // Normally you would delete the user from the database here
  res.status(204).send();
});
```

When a DELETE request is made to `http://localhost:3000/api/users/:id`, the server responds with a 204 No Content status, indicating successful deletion.

Combining HTTP Methods

Often, you'll want to create a unified route handler that manages different HTTP methods. Use the `.route()` method in Express to group these handlers together.

```
app.route('/api/users')
  .get((req, res) => {
    const users = [
      { id: 1, name: 'John Doe' },
      { id: 2, name: 'Jane Smith' }
    ];
    res.json(users);
  })
  .post((req, res) => {
    const newUser = {
      id: Date.now(),
      name: req.body.name
    };
    res.status(201).json(newUser);
  });

app.route('/api/users/:id')
  .put((req, res) => {
    const userId = req.params.id;
    const updatedUser = {
      id: userId,
      name: req.body.name
    };
    res.json(updatedUser);
  })
  .delete((req, res) => {
    const userId = req.params.id;
    res.status(204).send();
  });
```

Utilizing `.route()`, different HTTP methods can be conveniently managed under the same route path, improving code organization and readability.

Handling various HTTP methods is foundational to building robust and effective RESTful APIs. By correctly implementing these methods, your API will be able to handle common CRUD operations and offer a standard interface for interacting with resources.

8.4 Middleware in Routes

Middleware functions are a crucial part of building effective and maintainable applications with Express.js. They enable developers to modularize and separate their code, handling common tasks such as logging, authentication, and error handling. In this section, we will delve into how middleware can be used specifically within Express routes.

What is Middleware?

In the context of Express.js, middleware functions are functions that have access to the request object (req), the response object (res), and the next middleware function in the application's request-response cycle. Middleware functions can perform various tasks, such as executing code, modifying the request and response objects, ending the request-response cycle, or calling the next middleware function.

Here is a basic example of a middleware function:

```
function myMiddleware(req, res, next) {
    console.log('Middleware function executed');
    next(); // Pass control to the next middleware function
}
```

Using Middleware in Routes

There are multiple ways to apply middleware in Express routes. Middleware can be applied at the application level, router level, or directly within route definitions. The most common and flexible approach is to use middleware directly within route definitions.

Applying Middleware to a Single Route

You can use middleware functions within a specific route by providing the middleware function(s) as arguments before the route handler.

```javascript
const express = require('express');
const app = express();

function logRequest(req, res, next) {
    console.log(`${req.method} ${req.url}`);
    next();
}

app.get('http://localhost:3000/user', logRequest, (req, res
) => {
    res.send('User Profile');
});

app.listen(3000, () => {
    console.log('Server is running on http://localhost:3000
');
});
```

In this example, the logRequest middleware logs the HTTP method and URL of all incoming requests to /user. This middleware is specific to the /user route.

Applying Multiple Middleware Functions

You can also apply multiple middleware functions to a single route. Simply include each middleware function as an argument before the route handler.

```
const checkAuth = (req, res, next) => {
    if (req.isAuthenticated()) {
        next();
    } else {
        res.status(401).send('Unauthorized');
    }
};

const logRequest = (req, res, next) => {
    console.log(`${req.method} ${req.url}`);
    next();
};

app.get('http://localhost:3000/dashboard', checkAuth, LogRe
quest, (req, res) => {
    res.send('Dashboard');
});
```

In this example, the checkAuth middleware verifies if the user is authenticated before allowing access to the /dashboard route. If the user is authenticated, the logRequest middleware then logs the request details.

Using Middleware with Router-Level Middleware

Express routers allow for more modular and maintainable code by grouping route handlers into separate modules. Middleware can be applied to these routers in the same way as application-level middleware.

```
const express = require('express');
const app = express();
const router = express.Router();

const logRequest = (req, res, next) => {
    console.log(`${req.method} ${req.url}`);
    next();
};

router.use(logRequest);

router.get('http://localhost:3000/profile', (req, res) => {
    res.send('User Profile');
});

router.get('http://localhost:3000/settings', (req, res) =>
{
    res.send('User Settings');
});

app.use(router);

app.listen(3000, () => {
    console.log('Server is running on http://localhost:3000
');
});
```

In this example, the logRequest middleware is applied to all routes defined within the router. This removes the need to specify the middleware on each individual route, enhancing code readability and maintenance.

Error-Handling Middleware

Express provides a specialized type of middleware function for error handling, which can be used to manage errors occuring in your route handlers or other middleware.

```
function errorHandler(err, req, res, next) {
    console.error(err.stack);
    res.status(500).send('Something broke!');
}

app.use(errorHandler);
```

In this setup, any errors that occur within the application will be passed to the errorHandler middleware, which logs the error stack and sends a generic error response to the client.

Using middleware within Express routes allows developers to create modular, reusable components that can handle a variety of tasks. By understanding how to properly use middleware, you can significantly improve the maintainability and scalability of your applications.

9. Connecting to a Database

9.1 Choosing a Database

Choosing the right database for your RESTful API is a crucial decision that can significantly impact the performance, scalability, and maintainability of your application. There are two primary categories of databases to consider: relational databases (SQL) and non-relational databases (NoSQL). Each has its own set of advantages and trade-offs. In this subchapter, we will explore the key considerations to help you choose the most suitable database for your Node.js application.

Relational Databases (SQL)

Relational databases organize data into tables with predefined schemas and are known for their ACID (Atomicity, Consistency, Isolation, Durability) properties. Some popular relational databases include:

- MySQL
- PostgreSQL
- SQLite
- Microsoft SQL Server

Advantages:

1. **Structured Data**: Ideal for applications requiring structured data and complex queries involving multiple tables, joins, and transactions.
2. **Data Integrity**: Ensures data accuracy and integrity using constraints, foreign keys, and normalization.
3. **Standardized Query Language**: Uses SQL (Structured Query Language) which is standardized and widely adopted.

Considerations:

- **Complexity**: Requires predefined schemas which could be less flexible for applications with evolving data structures.
- **Scalability**: Horizontal scaling can be challenging compared to NoSQL databases.

Example: Connecting to MySQL in Node.js

To connect to a MySQL database in Node.js, you can use the `mysql` package:

```
const mysql = require('mysql');

const connection = mysql.createConnection({
  host: 'localhost',
  user: 'root',
  password: 'yourpassword',
  database: 'yourdatabase'
});

connection.connect((err) => {
  if (err) {
    console.error('An error occurred while connecting to th
e DB');
    throw err;
  }
  console.log('Connected to the database');
});
```

Non-Relational Databases (NoSQL)

NoSQL databases store data in a variety of ways including key-value pairs, documents, columns, and graphs. They are designed to handle large volumes of unstructured or semi-structured data.

- MongoDB (Document)
- Redis (Key-Value)
- Cassandra (Column)

- Neo4j (Graph)

Advantages:

1. **Flexibility**: Schemaless data models allow for rapid development and iteration.
2. **Scalability**: Often easier to scale horizontally, which is ideal for large-scale applications and high-performance requirements.
3. **Variety**: Different types of NoSQL databases are optimized for different use cases, such as document storage, key-value caching, wide-column stores, and graph traversal.

Considerations:

- **Consistency**: May compromise on immediate consistency in favor of eventual consistency for better performance.

- **Complex Queries**: Lacks the advanced querying capabilities and relational joining features of SQL databases.

Example: Connecting to MongoDB in Node.js

To connect to a MongoDB database in Node.js, you can use the mongodb package:

```
const { MongoClient } = require('mongodb');

const url = 'mongodb://localhost:27017';
const dbName = 'mydatabase';
const client = new MongoClient(url, { useNewUrlParser: true
, useUnifiedTopology: true });

client.connect((err) => {
  if (err) {
    console.error('An error occurred while connecting to Mo
ngoDB');
    throw err;
  }
  console.log('Connected to MongoDB');
  const db = client.db(dbName);
  // Perform database operations here
});
```

Hybrid Approach

Sometimes, using both SQL and NoSQL databases in your application can yield the best results. This hybrid approach allows you to leverage the strengths of both types of databases where they fit best. For example, you might use a relational database for transactional data requiring strong consistency and a NoSQL database for real-time analytics that need to handle large volumes of data efficiently.

Conclusion

Selecting the right database for your Node.js application hinges on your specific use case. If your application demands complex transactions and data integrity, a relational database might be the best bet. On the other hand, if flexibility and scalability are your top priorities, a NoSQL database could be more suitable. Consider the nature of your data, access patterns, scalability requirements, and development timeline when making your choice. In the next subchapter, we will look at how to set up the database environment for both types of databases.

9.2 Setting Up the Database

In this subchapter, we will guide you through setting up the database for your RESTful API using Node.js. For this book, we will use MongoDB due to its flexibility, ease of use, and ability to handle large datasets. However, the general principles can be applied to other databases as well. By the end of this subchapter, you should have a MongoDB instance running and ready to be connected to your application.

Installing MongoDB

First, you'll need to install MongoDB. Depending on your operating system, follow the appropriate instructions below.

For Windows:

1. Download MongoDB from the official website: https://www.mongodb.com/try/download/community
2. Run the downloaded installer and follow the setup wizard.
3. Ensure the MongoDB Server and MongoDB Compass options are checked.
4. Complete the installation process.
5. Add the MongoDB bin directory path to the system's PATH environment variable.

For macOS:

1. Open your terminal.

2. Use Homebrew to install MongoDB:

    ```
    brew tap mongodb/brew
    brew install mongodb-community
    ```

3. Start the MongoDB service:

```
brew services start mongodb/brew/mongodb-community
```

For Linux:

1. Follow the installation guide for your specific Linux distribution on the MongoDB official documentation page: https://docs.mongodb.com/manual/administration/install-on-linux/

2. Start the MongoDB service by running:

```
sudo systemctl start mongod
```

Running MongoDB

Once MongoDB is installed, you can start the MongoDB server using the following command in your terminal or command prompt:

```
mongod
```

This will start the MongoDB server process and connect to the default database instance.

Creating a Database

With MongoDB running, open another terminal or command prompt window and start the MongoDB shell by entering:

```
mongo
```

The MongoDB shell allows you to interact with your databases. By default, MongoDB does not require authentication, and you can create a new database easily.

To create a new database called `mydb`, simply switch to it (MongoDB will create the database if it doesn't already exist):

```
use mydb
```

Creating Collections

Within `mydb`, you can create collections to store your data. Collections in MongoDB are equivalent to tables in relational databases.

To create a collection called `users`, use the following command:

```
db.createCollection("users")
```

You can verify that the collection has been created by running:

```
show collections
```

Inserting Documents

MongoDB stores data in documents, which are similar to JSON objects. Let's insert a sample document into the `users` collection.

```
db.users.insertOne({
    name: "John Doe",
    email: "john.doe@example.com",
    age: 28
})
```

Setting Up Mongoose (for Node.js)

To interact with MongoDB from your Node.js application, we will use Mongoose, an Object Data Modeling (ODM) library for MongoDB and Node.js.

1. First, install Mongoose via npm by running:

```
npm install mongoose
```

2. Now, create a `models` directory in your project root. Within this directory, create a new file called `user.js`:

```javascript
const mongoose = require('mongoose');

const userSchema = new mongoose.Schema({
    name: {
        type: String,
        required: true
    },
    email: {
        type: String,
        required: true,
        unique: true
    },
    age: {
        type: Number,
        required: true
    }
});

const User = mongoose.model('User', userSchema);

module.exports = User;
```

This `user.js` file defines the schema for user documents and creates a model that can be used to interact with the `users` collection.

By following these steps, you now have a MongoDB instance set up and ready to be connected to your Node.js application. In the next subchapter, we will cover how to establish this connection and interact with the database from your Node.js code.

9.3 Connecting Node.js to the Database

Now that we've chosen and set up our database, the next step is to establish a connection from our Node.js application. Proper database connection management is crucial for efficient and reliable application behavior. This subchapter will guide you through connecting your Node.js application to the database, specifically focusing on MongoDB and MySQL as examples.

Prerequisites

Before you proceed, ensure you have the following: - Node.js installed on your machine. - The database (MongoDB/MySQL) set up and running. - Necessary Node.js packages installed (we will cover installation).

Connecting to MongoDB

Installing MongoDB Driver

First, install the MongoDB driver for Node.js. You can do this using npm:

```
npm install mongodb
```

Creating a Connection

Create a file named db.js in your project directory to manage the database connection:

```javascript
const { MongoClient } = require('mongodb');

// Connection URL
const url = 'mongodb://localhost:27017';

// Database Name
const dbName = 'myDatabase';

// Create a new MongoClient
const client = new MongoClient(url, { useNewUrlParser: true
, useUnifiedTopology: true });

async function connect() {
  try {
    // Connect the client to the server
    await client.connect();
    console.log('Connected successfully to MongoDB');

    // Select the database
    const db = client.db(dbName);

    // Additional database operations can be performed here

    return db;
  } catch (err) {
    console.error(err);
  }
}

module.exports = connect;
```

To use this connection in another file, you can import it:

```javascript
const connect = require('./db');

async function fetchData() {
  const db = await connect();
  // Your database logic here
}

fetchData();
```

Connecting to MySQL

Installing MySQL Driver

First, install the MySQL driver for Node.js:

```
npm install mysql
```

Creating a Connection

Create a file named db.js in your project directory to handle the MySQL connection:

```javascript
const mysql = require('mysql');

// Connection details
const connection = mysql.createConnection({
  host: 'localhost',
  user: 'yourUsername',
  password: 'yourPassword',
  database: 'myDatabase'
});

function connect() {
  return new Promise((resolve, reject) => {
    connection.connect((err) => {
      if (err) {
        console.error('Error connecting to MySQL:', err.sta
ck);
        return reject(err);
      }
      console.log('Connected to MySQL as id ' + connection.
threadId);
      resolve(connection);
    });
  });
}

module.exports = connect;
```

To use this connection in another file, you can import it:

```
const connect = require('./db');

async function fetchData() {
  const connection = await connect();

  connection.query('SELECT * FROM myTable', (error, results
, fields) => {
    if (error) throw error;
    console.log(results);
  });
}

fetchData();
```

Handling Connection Errors

Handling connection errors is vital for the stability of your application. Here are some strategies for both MongoDB and MySQL.

MongoDB Error Handling

In the MongoDB connection example above, errors are caught using a try...catch block. You can further handle errors by logging them or sending notifications:

```
async function connect() {
  try {
    await client.connect();
    console.log('Connected successfully to MongoDB');
    const db = client.db(dbName);
    return db;
  } catch (err) {
    console.error('MongoDB connection error:', err);
    // Additional error handling (logging, notifications, e
tc.)
  }
}
```

MySQL Error Handling

For MySQL, ensure that the promise returned by the `connect` function handles rejections:

```
function connect() {
  return new Promise((resolve, reject) => {
    connection.connect((err) => {
      if (err) {
        console.error('Error connecting to MySQL:', err.sta
ck);
        // Additional error handling (logging, notification
s, etc.)
        return reject(err);
      }
      console.log('Connected to MySQL as id ' + connection.
threadId);
      resolve(connection);
    });
  });
}
```

Closing Connections

Always close the database connection when it's no longer needed to avoid memory leaks and other potential issues.

Closing MongoDB Connection

```
async function close() {
  await client.close();
  console.log('MongoDB connection closed');
}
```

Closing MySQL Connection

```
connection.end((err) => {
  if (err) {
    console.error('Error closing MySQL connection:', err.st
ack);
    return;
  }
  console.log('MySQL connection closed');
});
```

By following these steps, you can successfully connect your Node.js application to a MongoDB or MySQL database, handle possible connection errors, and ensure that connections are appropriately closed, enhancing the reliability and performance of your application.

9.4 Handling Database Connections and Errors

Establishing and managing database connections efficiently is paramount for any application's stability and performance. In this subchapter, we will delve into handling database connections and errors strategically to ensure resilience and reliability in your RESTful APIs built with Node.js.

Connection Pooling

Connection pooling is a technique used to maintain a cache of database connections, allowing your application to reuse or share them rather than opening and closing connections repeatedly. This mechanism leads to improved performance and resource utilization.

Here's an example of setting up a connection pool using the popular `mysql` library for MySQL databases:

```
const mysql = require('mysql');

const pool = mysql.createPool({
  connectionLimit: 10,      // Maximum number of connections
in the pool
  host: 'localhost',
  user: 'root',
  password: 'password',
  database: 'mydatabase'
});

pool.getConnection((err, connection) => {
  if (err) {
    console.error('Error getting MySQL connection:', err);
    return;
  }

  // Use the connection
  connection.query('SELECT * FROM users', (error, results)
=> {
    // Release the connection back to the pool
    connection.release();

    if (error) {
      console.error('Error executing query:', error);
      return;
    }

    console.log('User data:', results);
  });
});
```

Managing Errors

Handling errors gracefully in database operations prevents your application from crashing and provides meaningful feedback to the end-users.

Connection Errors

Connection errors can occur due to incorrect credentials, server downtime, or network issues. Here is how you can handle such errors:

```
pool.getConnection((err, connection) => {
  if (err) {
    if (err.code === 'PROTOCOL_CONNECTION_LOST') {
      console.error('Database connection was closed.');
    }
    if (err.code === 'ER_CON_COUNT_ERROR') {
      console.error('Database has too many connections.');
    }
    if (err.code === 'ECONNREFUSED') {
      console.error('Database connection was refused.');
    }
  }

  if (connection) connection.release();

  return;
});
```

Query Errors

When executing queries, handling errors ensures that any issues are logged and handled without impacting your application's user experience:

```
pool.query('SELECT * FROM non_existing_table', (error, resu
lts) => {
  if (error) {
    console.error('Error executing query:', error);
    // Handle the error appropriately
    return;
  }

  console.log('Results:', results);
});
```

Graceful Shutdown

When your application shuts down, it is essential to close all database connections gracefully to avoid any potential data loss or corruption.

```
const exitHandler = () => {
  pool.end(err => {
    if (err) {
      console.error('Error closing MySQL pool:', err);
    } else {
      console.log('MySQL pool closed.');
    }

    process.exit();
  });
};

// Capture termination signals
process.on('SIGINT', exitHandler);
process.on('SIGTERM', exitHandler);
```

Retrying Connections

Intermittent network issues can cause temporary connection failures. Implementing a retry mechanism can improve your application's resilience.

```
function connectWithRetry() {
  pool.getConnection((err, connection) => {
    if (err) {
      console.error('Error getting MySQL connection:', err)
;
      setTimeout(connectWithRetry, 5000); // Retry after 5
seconds
      return;
    }

    console.log('Connected to MySQL database.');
    if (connection) connection.release();
  });
}

connectWithRetry();
```

Summary

Effective handling of database connections and errors involves using connection pooling, managing different types of errors, implementing graceful shutdown procedures, and introducing retry mechanisms for connection attempts. These practices help ensure that your application remains stable, performs optimally, and provides a reliable experience to users.

10. Handling Authentication and Authorization

10.1 Introduction to Authentication and Authorization

In the modern web development landscape, securing your application and its data is of paramount importance. This is achieved through robust authentication and authorization mechanisms. Understanding and implementing these concepts correctly is particularly crucial when building RESTful APIs with Node.js as these mechanisms ensure that only authorized users can access or manipulate resources.

What is Authentication?

Authentication is the process of verifying the identity of a user or system. In the context of a RESTful API, authentication is typically implemented to ensure that the requests being made to the API are from legitimate users or systems. This can be achieved through various methods such as API keys, OAuth, and JSON Web Tokens (JWT).

Example of Basic Authentication

Basic authentication involves sending a username and password with each request. Here is a simple example in the context of an Express.js application:

```javascript
const express = require('express');
const app = express();

const basicAuth = (req, res, next) => {
  const authHeader = req.headers['authorization'];
  if (!authHeader) {
    return res.status(401).json({ message: 'Missing Authori
zation Header' });
  }

  const base64Credentials = authHeader.split(' ')[1];
  const credentials = Buffer.from(base64Credentials, 'base6
4').toString('ascii');
  const [username, password] = credentials.split(':');

  if (username === 'admin' && password === 'secret') {
    next();
  } else {
    res.status(401).json({ message: 'Invalid Credentials' }
);
  }
};

app.get('/secure-endpoint', basicAuth, (req, res) => {
  res.json({ message: 'This is a secure endpoint' });
});

app.listen(3000, () => {
  console.log('Server running at http://localhost:3000');
});
```

In this example, basicAuth middleware checks for the presence of an Authorization header, decodes it, and verifies the provided credentials.

What is Authorization?

Authorization comes into play once the user is authenticated. It is the process of determining whether the authenticated user has the necessary permissions to perform a specific action or access a particular resource. Authorization is crucial for implementing Role-Based Access Control (RBAC), where different users have different levels of access to resources.

Example of Role-Based Authorization

Role-based authorization can be implemented by assigning roles to users and then checking these roles before granting access:

```
const roles = {
  admin: ['read', 'write', 'delete'],
  user: ['read']
};

const authorize = (role, action) => {
  return (req, res, next) => {
    const userRole = req.headers['role'];
    if (roles[userRole] && roles[userRole].includes(action)
) {
      next();
    } else {
      res.status(403).json({ message: 'Forbidden' });
    }
  };
};

app.get('/admin-endpoint', authorize('admin', 'read'), (req
, res) => {
  res.json({ message: 'This is an admin endpoint' });
});

app.get('/user-endpoint', authorize('user', 'read'), (req,
res) => {
  res.json({ message: 'This is a user endpoint' });
});
```

In this script, the `authorize` middleware checks the user's role and grants or denies access based on the action they are attempting to perform.

Why Both Matter

While authentication is the gatekeeper ensuring that systems know who the user is, authorization determines what an authenticated user can do. Implementing these correctly helps in:

1. **Data Security:** Ensures that only authorized users can access sensitive data.

2. **Operational Security:** Limits actions that users can perform, thus reducing inadvertent or malicious damage.

3. **Compliance:** Helps in meeting regulatory requirements for data privacy and access controls.

Conclusion

Understanding and correctly implementing authentication and authorization mechanisms is crucial when building secure and robust RESTful APIs with Node.js. In the following sections of this chapter, we will delve deeper into specific techniques and tools, such as JSON Web Tokens (JWT) and middleware, to aid in the secure implementation of these concepts.

10.2 Implementing JSON Web Tokens (JWT)

Implementing JSON Web Tokens (JWT) is a crucial step in securing RESTful APIs. JWTs offer an efficient and compact way to represent claims between two parties, typically between a server and a client. They enable stateless authentication, eliminating the need for server-side sessions. In this subchapter, we explore how to implement JWT in a Node.js application.

What is a JWT?

A JSON Web Token (JWT) is a compact, URL-safe token that consists of three parts: 1. **Header**: Contains metadata about the token, including the type and the signing algorithm. 2. **Payload**: Contains the claims or data you wish to include in the token. 3. **Signature**: Ensures the token hasn't been altered. It's a combination of the header, payload, and a secret key, all run through a cryptographic algorithm.

These parts are base64 encoded and concatenated with periods ('.') to form the JWT.

Why Use JWT?

- **Stateless Authentication**: Eliminates the need for server-side sessions, making the system stateless and more scalable.
- **Compact**: Small in size, making it ideal for usage in a URL or HTTP header.
- **Self-contained**: Contains all the information needed to understand and verify the token itself.

Setting Up JWT in a Node.js Application

Let's walk through the process of implementing JWT in a Node.js application using the jsonwebtoken library.

Installing Dependencies

First, install the necessary npm package:

```
npm install jsonwebtoken
```

Creating and Signing a JWT

To create and sign a JWT, you need a secret key. This key is used to generate the token's signature.

```javascript
const jwt = require('jsonwebtoken');

const user = {
  id: 1,
  username: 'exampleUser'
};

// Replace 'your-256-bit-secret' with your actual secret key
const secretKey = 'your-256-bit-secret';

const token = jwt.sign(user, secretKey, { expiresIn: '1h' });

console.log('Generated Token:', token);
```

In this example, a token is generated for a user object and is set to expire in one hour.

Verifying a JWT

To verify the authenticity of a JWT, you need to use the same secret key that was used to sign it.

```javascript
const receivedToken = '...'; // Replace with your received
or generated token

try {
  const decoded = jwt.verify(receivedToken, secretKey);
  console.log('Decoded Token:', decoded);
} catch (error) {
  console.error('Token verification failed:', error.message
);
}
```

Middleware for Securing Endpoints

To secure your API endpoints with JWT, create a middleware function that verifies the token.

```
const express = require('express');
const app = express();

const authenticateJWT = (req, res, next) => {
  const authHeader = req.headers.authorization;

  if (authHeader) {
    const token = authHeader.split(' ')[1];

    jwt.verify(token, secretKey, (err, user) => {
      if (err) {
        return res.sendStatus(403);
      }

      req.user = user;
      next();
    });
  } else {
    res.sendStatus(401);
  }
};

// Applying the middleware to secure a route
app.get('/protected', authenticateJWT, (req, res) => {
  res.json({ message: 'This is a protected route.', user: r
eq.user });
});

app.listen(3000, () => {
  console.log('Server running on http://localhost:3000');
});
```

Adding JWT to User Authentication Flow

A common flow might involve the user logging in, the server verifying the credentials, and then issuing a token.

```
const express = require('express');
const bodyParser = require('body-parser');
const app = express();

app.use(bodyParser.json());

const users = [
  {
    id: 1,
    username: 'exampleUser',
    password: 'password'
  }
];

app.post('/Login', (req, res) => {
  const { username, password } = req.body;
  const user = users.find(u => u.username === username && u
.password === password);

  if (user) {
    const token = jwt.sign({ id: user.id, username: user.us
ername }, secretKey, { expiresIn: '1h' });
    res.json({ token });
  } else {
    res.status(401).json({ message: 'Invalid credentials' }
);
  }
});

app.listen(3000, () => {
  console.log('Server running on http://localhost:3000');
});
```

In this flow: 1. The client sends a POST request to /login with username and password. 2. The server verifies the credentials, and if valid, generates a token. 3. The token is sent back to the client for use in future authenticated requests.

Conclusion

JWTs provide a robust and scalable solution for securing your RESTful APIs. By incorporating JWTs into your Node.js application, you can ensure a secure and seamless authentication process. Proceed to the next subchapter to learn how to secure your endpoints with middleware.

10.3 Securing Endpoints with Middleware

In Chapter 7, "Middleware Functions," we discussed the essential role middleware plays in an Express.js application. Middleware can be effectively utilized to secure your API endpoints by intercepting incoming requests and ensuring they meet specific security requirements before proceeding to route handlers. In this section, we will focus on how to secure endpoints using middleware to handle authentication and authorization.

Understanding Middleware for Security

Middleware functions are invoked before the actual route handlers. This makes them ideal for implementing security measures like checking for valid tokens, permissions, or roles. As a security best practice, you should place your middleware functions before your routes to ensure every incoming request is validated and authorized.

Implementing Authentication Middleware

Authentication middleware is responsible for verifying that the incoming request is from a legitimate user. One of the most common methods for authenticating API requests in modern applications involves the use of JSON Web Tokens (JWT). We already covered JWTs in the previous section, so let's put this into practice by creating an authentication middleware.

```
const jwt = require('jsonwebtoken');

function authenticateToken(req, res, next) {
    const authHeader = req.headers['authorization'];
    const token = authHeader && authHeader.split(' ')[1];

    if (token == null) return res.sendStatus(401); // Unaut
horized

    jwt.verify(token, process.env.ACCESS_TOKEN_SECRET, (err
, user) => {
        if (err) return res.sendStatus(403); // Forbidden
        req.user = user;
        next();
    });
}

module.exports = authenticateToken;
```

Here's how to use this middleware in your route definitions:

```
const express = require('express');
const app = express();
const authenticateToken = require('./middleware/authenticat
eToken');

app.get('http://example.com/api/protected', authenticateTok
en, (req, res) => {
    res.json({ message: 'This is a protected route', user:
req.user });
});

app.listen(3000);
```

Any request to `http://example.com/api/protected` will first pass through the `authenticateToken` middleware. If the token is valid, the user is granted access; otherwise, the request is denied.

Implementing Authorization Middleware

After authentication, the next step is ensuring the authenticated user has the required permissions to access a particular resource. This process is known as authorization. You might want to implement Role-Based Access Control (RBAC) or a more granular permissions-based system, as discussed in the next section (10.4 Role-Based Access Control).

Here's an example of an authorization middleware function that checks for a specific role:

```
function authorizeRole(role) {
    return (req, res, next) => {
        if (req.user.role !== role) {
            return res.sendStatus(403); // Forbidden
        }
        next();
    };
}

module.exports = authorizeRole;
```

To apply this middleware, it can be added to your route definitions like so:

```
const express = require('express');
const app = express();
const authenticateToken = require('./middleware/authenticateToken');
const authorizeRole = require('./middleware/authorizeRole');

app.get('http://example.com/admin', authenticateToken, authorizeRole('admin'), (req, res) => {
    res.json({ message: 'Welcome Admin' });
});

app.listen(3000);
```

In this example, only users with the role of 'admin' can access the `http://example.com/admin` endpoint.

Combining Authentication and Authorization Middleware

In practice, you often need to combine multiple middleware functions to ensure both authentication and authorization in a single request process. This is achieved by chaining multiple middleware functions.

```
const express = require('express');
const app = express();
const authenticateToken = require('./middleware/authenticat
eToken');
const authorizeRole = require('./middleware/authorizeRole')
;

app.get('http://example.com/admin', authenticateToken, auth
orizeRole('admin'), (req, res) => {
    res.json({ message: 'Welcome Admin' });
});

app.get('http://example.com/user', authenticateToken, autho
rizeRole('user'), (req, res) => {
    res.json({ message: 'Welcome User' });
});

app.listen(3000);
```

This approach makes it easy to manage security across different endpoints by composing middleware chains that handle specific security needs.

Conclusion

Securing API endpoints with middleware is a robust way to both authenticate and authorize users in your application. By leveraging JWTs for authentication and composing authorization checks, you can build a flexible and secure API. In the next section, we will delve deeper into Role-Based Access Control (RBAC) to enhance our authorization strategy further.

10.4 Role-Based Access Control (RBAC)

Role-Based Access Control (RBAC) is a method of regulating access to resources based on the roles of individual users within an organization. In the context of RESTful APIs with Node.js, RBAC helps in restricting certain actions and data based on user roles. This section will walk you through the process of implementing RBAC in your Node.js API.

Understanding RBAC

RBAC assigns permissions to specific roles rather than to individual users. Users are then assigned roles, and they inherit the permissions associated with those roles. This approach simplifies the management of permissions, especially in systems with a large number of users.

Defining Roles and Permissions

First, let's define the roles and their associated permissions. For the sake of illustration, consider an API with three primary roles: admin, editor, and viewer. An admin has full control, an editor can modify content, and a viewer has read-only access.

Create a file named roles.js to define the roles and their permissions:

```
const roles = {
  admin: ['read', 'write', 'delete'],
  editor: ['read', 'write'],
  viewer: ['read']
};

module.exports = roles;
```

Adding Roles to Users

Assume that you have a user model where you store user details including their roles. Here's an example user schema using Mongoose:

```
const mongoose = require('mongoose');
const Schema = mongoose.Schema;

const userSchema = new Schema({
  username: { type: String, required: true, unique: true },
  password: { type: String, required: true },
  role: { type: String, enum: ['admin', 'editor', 'viewer']
, default: 'viewer' }
});

const User = mongoose.model('User', userSchema);
module.exports = User;
```

Middleware to Check Permissions

To enforce RBAC, you need middleware that checks if a user has the appropriate role to access a specific endpoint.

Create a file named checkRole.js:

```
const roles = require('./roles');

const checkRole = (role) => {
  return (req, res, next) => {
    if (!req.user) {
      return res.status(401).json({ message: 'Unauthorized'
});
    }

    const userRole = req.user.role;
    const permissions = roles[userRole];

    if (!permissions || !permissions.includes(role)) {
      return res.status(403).json({ message: 'Forbidden' })
;
    }

    next();
  };
};

module.exports = checkRole;
```

Protecting Routes with RBAC

With the checkRole middleware in place, you can now protect your routes. Here's an example using Express:

```
const express = require('express');
const app = express();
const checkRole = require('./middlewares/checkRole');
const jwtAuth = require('./middlewares/jwtAuth');  // Middl
eware to validate JWT and set req.user

app.use(jwtAuth);  // Ensure JWT token validation is applie
d to all routes

app.get('/admin', checkRole('admin'), (req, res) => {
  res.json({ message: 'Admin content' });
});

app.post('/edit', checkRole('write'), (req, res) => {
  res.json({ message: 'Editor content' });
});

app.get('/view', checkRole('read'), (req, res) => {
  res.json({ message: 'Viewer content' });
});

const PORT = process.env.PORT || 3000;
app.listen(PORT, () => {
  console.log(`Server is running on port ${PORT}`);
});
```

Handling User Roles During Authentication

When handling user authentication, ensure that the JWT token includes the user's role information. Here's an example of an authentication endpoint:

```
const express = require('express');
const jwt = require('jsonwebtoken');
const User = require('./models/user');
const bcrypt = require('bcrypt');

const app = express();

app.post('/login', async (req, res) => {
  const { username, password } = req.body;

  const user = await User.findOne({ username });
  if (!user) {
    return res.status(401).json({ message: 'Invalid credent
ials' });
  }

  const match = await bcrypt.compare(password, user.passwor
d);
  if (!match) {
    return res.status(401).json({ message: 'Invalid credent
ials' });
  }

  const token = jwt.sign(
    { id: user._id, role: user.role },
    'your_jwt_secret',
    { expiresIn: '1h' }
  );

  res.json({ token });
});

const PORT = process.env.PORT || 3000;
app.listen(PORT, () => {
  console.log(`Server is running on port ${PORT}`);
});
```

Conclusion

Implementing Role-Based Access Control (RBAC) in your Node.js RESTful API allows you to efficiently manage access to different parts of your application based on user roles. By defining roles and permissions, adding roles to user objects, and creating middleware to enforce these roles, you can ensure that your application remains secure and organized.

11. Testing and Debugging

11.1 Unit Testing

Unit testing is a crucial aspect of software development, and it plays an essential role in ensuring that each individual component of your RESTful API functions as expected. By focusing on testing the smallest testable parts of your application, we can catch and fix bugs at the early stages of development, thereby reducing the likelihood of encountering serious issues later on.

What is Unit Testing?

Unit testing involves testing individual units or components of your code to verify that each part functions correctly. In the context of a Node.js RESTful API, a unit could be a single function, a method, or an endpoint handler. These tests are typically automated and are written in tandem with the code they are testing.

Benefits of Unit Testing

1. **Early Bug Detection**: By testing individual units, you can detect and fix bugs early in the development cycle.

2. **Code Refactoring**: Unit tests provide a safety net that allows you to refactor code without fear of introducing new bugs.

3. **Documentation**: Unit tests act as a form of documentation that helps other developers understand what the code is supposed to do.

4. **Simplifies Integration**: When combined with integration tests, unit tests help ensure that individual components work together smoothly.

Setting Up Your Testing Environment

To start unit testing your Node.js application, you'll need a testing framework. Popular choices include Mocha, Jest, and Jasmine. For this example, we'll use Jest due to its simplicity and rich feature set.

1. **Install Jest**: First, install Jest using npm.

   ```
   npm install --save-dev jest
   ```

2. **Update package.json**: Add a test script to your package.json file.

   ```
   "scripts": {
     "test": "jest"
   }
   ```

Writing Your First Unit Test

Consider a basic utility function that needs to be tested:

```
// utils/math.js
function add(a, b) {
    return a + b;
}

module.exports = add;
```

Create a test file for the add function:

```
// tests/math.test.js
const add = require('../utils/math');

test('adds 1 + 2 to equal 3', () => {
    expect(add(1, 2)).toBe(3);
});
```

Run the tests using:

```
npm test
```

Testing API Endpoints

For testing API endpoints, you can use a combination of Jest and Supertest. Let's say you have an Express route that you want to test:

```
// routes/user.js
const express = require('express');
const router = express.Router();

router.get('/user/:id', (req, res) => {
    const userId = req.params.id;
    res.status(200).json({ id: userId, name: 'John Doe' });
});

module.exports = router;
```

To test this endpoint:

1. **Create a Test File**:

```
// tests/user.test.js
const request = require('supertest');
const express = require('express');
const userRouter = require('../routes/user');

const app = express();
app.use('/api', userRouter);

test('GET /api/user/:id should return user data', async () => {
    const userId = '123';
    const response = await request(app).get(`/api/user/${userId}`);
    expect(response.status).toBe(200);
    expect(response.body).toEqual({ id: userId, name: 'John Doe' });
});
```

2. **Run the Test**:

```
npm test
```

Mocking Dependencies

Mocking is useful when your unit tests depend on external services or modules. For example, if your endpoint fetches data from a database, you can mock the database calls.

```
// models/userModel.js
const getUserById = async (id) => {
    // Imagine this function fetches user data from a datab
ase
    return { id, name: 'John Doe' };
};

module.exports = { getUserById };
```

To test the endpoint without depending on a real database:

1. **Mock the Module**:

    ```
    // tests/user.test.js
    const request = require('supertest');
    const express = require('express');
    const userRouter = require('../routes/user');
    const userModel = require('../models/userModel');

    jest.mock('../models/userModel');

    const app = express();
    app.use('/api', userRouter);

    test('GET /api/user/:id should return user data', asy
    nc () => {
        const userId = '123';
        userModel.getUserById.mockResolvedValue({ id: use
    rId, name: 'John Doe' });

        const response = await request(app).get(`/api/use
    r/${userId}`);
        expect(response.status).toBe(200);
        expect(response.body).toEqual({ id: userId, name:
    'John Doe' });
    });
    ```

Best Practices

1. **Isolate Tests**: Unit tests should be independent and isolated from each other.

2. **Keep Tests Fast**: Ensure your unit tests run quickly to facilitate frequent testing.

3. **Meaningful Names**: Use descriptive names for your test cases to make them self-explanatory.

4. **Consistent Structure**: Maintain a consistent file structure for your tests, mirroring the structure of your application code.

By incorporating unit testing into your development workflow, you can create a more robust, maintainable, and high-quality RESTful API with Node.js.

11.2 Integration Testing

Integration testing is a crucial phase in the testing lifecycle of your RESTful API. It verifies the interactions between different modules of the application, ensuring they work together as expected. Unlike unit testing, which isolates individual components, integration testing focuses on the interoperability of multiple units, uncovering issues that may arise when they are combined.

The Importance of Integration Testing

Integration testing helps to uncover issues related to data flow and control among various modules. It ensures that: - The interaction between different modules is functioning correctly. - Data across different components is shared and manipulated as expected. - The combined functionality meets the requirements.

In the context of a RESTful API, integration tests typically simulate HTTP requests and validate the responses to ensure the API's endpoints work correctly together.

Setting Up Integration Testing for Your API

To perform integration testing in a Node.js environment, you will need a testing framework. Popular choices include Mocha, Chai, and Supertest. Below is an example setup using these tools.

First, install the necessary packages:

```
npm install --save-dev mocha chai supertest
```

Writing Integration Tests

Create a file named `integration.test.js` in your test directory. Below is a basic example of integration tests for an API that manages a collection of books.

Example API Endpoints

- Create a new book: POST `http://localhost:3000/books`
- Get the book list: GET `http://localhost:3000/books`
- Get a specific book by ID: GET `http://localhost:3000/books/:id`
- Update a book: PUT `http://localhost:3000/books/:id`
- Delete a book: DELETE `http://localhost:3000/books/:id`

Sample Data

```
{
  "title": "Node.js Design Patterns",
  "author": "Mario Casciaro",
  "year": 2014
}
```

Integration Test Implementation

Here is how to write integration tests for the above endpoints:

```javascript
const chai = require('chai');
const chaiHttp = require('chai-http');
const app = require('../app'); // Assuming your Express app
is exported from this file.
const expect = chai.expect;

chai.use(chaiHttp);

describe('Books API Integration Tests', () => {
  let bookId;

  // Test creating a new book
  it('should create a new book', (done) => {
    chai.request(app)
      .post('http://localhost:3000/books')
      .send({ title: 'Node.js Design Patterns', author: 'Ma
rio Casciaro', year: 2014 })
      .end((err, res) => {
        expect(res).to.have.status(201);
        expect(res.body).to.be.an('object');
        expect(res.body).to.include.keys('_id', 'title', 'a
uthor', 'year');
        bookId = res.body._id;
        done();
      });
  });

  // Test retrieving the book list
  it('should retrieve the book list', (done) => {
    chai.request(app)
      .get('http://localhost:3000/books')
      .end((err, res) => {
        expect(res).to.have.status(200);
        expect(res.body).to.be.an('array');
        done();
      });
  });

  // Test retrieving a specific book by ID
  it('should retrieve a book by ID', (done) => {
    chai.request(app)
      .get(`http://localhost:3000/books/${bookId}`)
      .end((err, res) => {
        expect(res).to.have.status(200);
        expect(res.body).to.be.an('object');
        expect(res.body).to.include.keys('_id', 'title', 'a
uthor', 'year');
```

```
      done();
    });
  });

  // Test updating a book
  it('should update a book', (done) => {
    chai.request(app)
      .put(`http://localhost:3000/books/${bookId}`)
      .send({ author: 'Mario Casciaro & Luciano Mammino' })
      .end((err, res) => {
        expect(res).to.have.status(200);
        expect(res.body).to.be.an('object');
        expect(res.body.author).to.equal('Mario Casciaro &
Luciano Mammino');
        done();
      });
  });

  // Test deleting a book
  it('should delete a book', (done) => {
    chai.request(app)
      .delete(`http://localhost:3000/books/${bookId}`)
      .end((err, res) => {
        expect(res).to.have.status(204);
        done();
      });
  });
  });
});
```

Running the Integration Tests

You can run the integration tests using Mocha. Add a test script in
your package.json:

```
{
  "scripts": {
    "test": "mocha"
  }
}
```

Then run the tests using:

```
npm test
```

The output should be a series of passes or failures based on the interactions between the different modules of your API.

Conclusion

Integration testing ensures that your RESTful API operates as expected when different application modules interact. Through proper setup and execution of integration tests, you can detect and resolve issues that unit tests may not catch, leading to a more robust and reliable application.

11.3 Debugging Techniques

Debugging is an essential part of the development process, especially when building RESTful APIs with Node.js. Identifying and fixing errors ensure that your API runs smoothly and handles requests as expected. This subchapter covers various debugging techniques and tools that can help you diagnose and resolve issues effectively.

Understanding Common Issues

Before diving into specific debugging techniques, it's crucial to understand the common types of problems you might encounter:

- **Syntax Errors**: These are errors in your code syntax and are usually flagged by the development environment or during compilation.

- **Runtime Errors**: These errors occur when your code attempts to execute an invalid operation (e.g., accessing a property on an undefined object).

- **Logical Errors**: These are mistakes in the logic of your code. Unlike syntax and runtime errors, they do not generally trigger error messages but result in incorrect behavior.

Using `console.log`

One of the simplest and most common debugging methods is using `console.log()` to print variables and messages to the console. This technique can help you trace the flow of your code and inspect values at various stages.

```
app.get('/api/users/:id', (req, res) => {
  const userId = req.params.id;
  console.log(`Fetching user with ID: ${userId}`);

  // Simulating a user fetch
  const user = { id: userId, name: 'John Doe' };
  console.log('User data:', user);

  res.json(user);
});
```

Using Debuggers

A more robust method involves using a debugger tool to set breakpoints, step through code, inspect variables, and evaluate expressions.

Node.js Built-In Debugger

Node.js comes with a built-in debugger that can be invoked using the `inspect` flag.

1. Start your application with the debugger:

```
node --inspect-brk server.js
```

6. Open `chrome://inspect` in Google Chrome to connect to your running application.

7. From the DevTools interface, you can set breakpoints, step through your code, and inspect variables.

Visual Studio Code (VSCode) Debugger

If you're using VSCode, you can leverage its integrated debugger.

1. Add a configuration for Node.js in the `launch.json` file:

```
{
  "version": "0.2.0",
  "configurations": [
    {
      "type": "node",
      "request": "launch",
      "name": "Launch Program",
      "program": "${workspaceFolder}/server.js",
      "skipFiles": ["<node_internals>/**"]
    }
  ]
}
```

2. Set breakpoints directly in your code by clicking in the gutter next to the line you want to break on.

3. Run the debugger by pressing F5 or by clicking the green play button in the Debug panel.

Using Node.js Debugging Tools

There are several third-party debugging tools and libraries that can assist you:

- **nodemon**: Automatically restarts your Node.js application when file changes in the directory are detected.

```
npm install -g nodemon
nodemon server.js
```

- **debug**: A small debugging utility for Node.js, commonly used in various Node.js libraries.

```
npm install debug
```

Use it in your code:

```
const debug = require('debug')('app');

app.get('/api/users/:id', (req, res) => {
  const userId = req.params.id;
  debug(`Fetching user with ID: ${userId}`);

  // Simulating a user fetch
  const user = { id: userId, name: 'John Doe' };
  debug('User data:', user);

  res.json(user);
});
```

Run your application with the DEBUG environment variable:

```
DEBUG=app node server.js
```

Catching Unhandled Errors

To catch unhandled errors and prevent your application from crashing, you can use error-handling middleware in Express or process-level error handlers.

Express Error-Handling Middleware

```
app.use((err, req, res, next) => {
  console.error('Error:', err.message);
  res.status(500).json({ error: 'Internal Server Error' });
});
```

Process-Level Error Handlers

```
process.on('uncaughtException', (err) => {
  console.error('Uncaught Exception:', err.message);
  // Perform any cleanup or logging
  process.exit(1);
});

process.on('unhandledRejection', (reason, promise) => {
  console.error('Unhandled Rejection:', reason.message);
  // Perform any cleanup or logging
});
```

Debugging Network Requests

When dealing with RESTful APIs, it's also essential to debug network requests to verify that they are being sent and received correctly. Tools such as Postman and curl can be invaluable.

Using Postman

Postman is a powerful tool for API testing that allows you to send HTTP requests and view responses.

1. Download and install Postman from `https://www.postman.com/downloads/`.

2. Create a new request, specify the HTTP method, enter the full URL (e.g., `http://localhost:3000/api/users`), and send the request.

3. Inspect the response to verify the data returned by your API.

Using curl

curl is a command-line tool for transferring data with URLs.

```
curl -X GET http://localhost:3000/api/users
```

This command sends a GET request to your API and prints the response to the console.

Conclusion

Effective debugging requires a combination of tools and techniques. Whether you're inserting `console.log()` statements or using sophisticated debugger tools, the goal is to gain insights into your application's behavior and resolve issues efficiently. By mastering these debugging techniques, you'll be better equipped to build robust and reliable RESTful APIs with Node.js.

11.4 Mocking and Stubbing

In the realm of testing and debugging, particularly in the context of building RESTful APIs with Node.js, mocking and stubbing are essential techniques. These methods allow developers to isolate and test units of code in a controlled environment, ensuring they work correctly without dependencies influencing the results.

What is Mocking?

Mocking involves creating fake objects or functions that simulate the behavior of real components. Mocks are used to test the interactions between units of code, verifying that certain functions are called with the expected arguments. This is particularly useful when the real objects are challenging to create or manipulate.

Example of Mocking

Consider a scenario where you have a service that makes HTTP requests to an external API. During testing, you don't want to make actual HTTP requests. Instead, you create a mock of the HTTP request function.

```javascript
const { expect } = require('chai');
const sinon = require('sinon');
const axios = require('axios');
const myService = require('../path/to/myService');

describe('My Service', function() {
  it('should call external API', async function() {
    const mockResponse = { data: { userId: 1, id: 1, title:
'Mock title' } };
    const axiosStub = sinon.stub(axios, 'get').resolves(moc
kResponse);

    const result = await myService.fetchData();

    expect(axiosStub.calledOnce).to.be.true;
    expect(result).to.equal(mockResponse.data);

    axiosStub.restore();
  });
});
```

In this example, `sinon.stub` is used to replace the `axios.get` method with a mock that returns predefined data. This isolates the test from the actual external API.

What is Stubbing?

Stubbing is a specific type of mocking where the behavior of functions or methods is overridden. Stubs provide controlled responses when functions are called. Unlike mocks, stubs don't verify interactions directly but focus on providing certain return values or behaviors.

Example of Stubbing

Let's say you have a function that depends on a database call. During testing, you can stub the database method to return a specific value.

```
const { expect } = require('chai');
const sinon = require('sinon');
const database = require('../path/to/database');
const myService = require('../path/to/myService');

describe('My Service', function() {
  it('should return user data from database', async functio
n() {
    const userStub = { id: 1, name: 'John Doe' };
    sinon.stub(database, 'getUserById').resolves(userStub);

    const result = await myService.getUserData(1);

    expect(result).to.deep.equal(userStub);

    database.getUserById.restore();
  });
});
```

Here, `sinon.stub` is used to replace the `getUserById` function of the `database` module, ensuring that during the test, it returns the `userStub` object.

Using Mocking and Stubbing Together

Mocking and stubbing can be combined to create comprehensive unit tests that isolate even the most complex dependencies. For example, you might mock an HTTP request while stubbing several internal service functions.

```
const { expect } = require('chai');
const sinon = require('sinon');
const axios = require('axios');
const myService = require('../path/to/myService');
const database = require('../path/to/database');

describe('My Service', function() {
  beforeEach(function() {
    sinon.restore(); // Resets all stubs and mocks before each test
  });

  it('should process data and save to database', async function() {
    const mockResponse = { data: { userId: 1, id: 1, title: 'Mock title' } };
    const processedData = { userId: 1, title: 'Processed Mock title' };

    sinon.stub(axios, 'get').resolves(mockResponse);
    sinon.stub(myService, 'processData').returns(processedData);
    const saveStub = sinon.stub(database, 'saveData').resolves({ success: true });

    const result = await myService.fetchAndSaveData();

    expect(axios.get.calledOnce).to.be.true;
    expect(myService.processData.calledOnceWith(mockResponse.data)).to.be.true;
    expect(saveStub.calledOnceWith(processedData)).to.be.true;
    expect(result.success).to.be.true;
  });
});
```

In this example, `axios.get` is mocked to return pre-defined data, `myService.processData` is stubbed to return a modified version of that data, and `database.saveData` is stubbed to simulate a successful save operation. This test ensures each component works correctly in isolation.

Conclusion

Mocking and stubbing are powerful techniques for writing robust, isolated tests in a Node.js environment. By using tools like Sinon, you can create mocks and stubs that help validate your code's behavior without relying on real external dependencies, making your tests faster, more reliable, and easier to execute. These techniques are crucial for maintaining a high standard of code quality and facilitating smooth development and debugging processes.

12. Glossary

Glossary

API (Application Programming Interface)

A set of rules and protocols for building and interacting with software applications. It defines the kinds of calls or requests that can be made, how to make them, the data formats that should be used, and the conventions to follow.

REST (Representational State Transfer)

An architectural style for designing networked applications. RESTful systems typically communicate over HTTP, using simple verbs such as GET, POST, PUT, and DELETE. They are stateless and rely on standardized URIs.

Node.js

A server-side platform built on Google Chrome's JavaScript Engine (V8 Engine). Node.js is designed to build scalable network applications.

Express.js

A web application framework for Node.js, designed for building web applications and APIs. It is the standard server framework for Node.js.

Middleware

Functions that execute during the lifecycle of a request to the Express server. Middleware functions have access to the request object (req), the response object (res), and the next middleware function in the application's request-response cycle.

Routing

The process of defining how an application responds to a client request to a particular endpoint, which is a URI (or path) and a specific HTTP request method (GET, POST, PUT, DELETE, etc.).

URI (Uniform Resource Identifier)

A string of characters used to identify a resource on the Internet, which includes URLs (Uniform Resource Locators) as a subset.

HTTP Methods

Methods defined in HTTP used to perform actions on resources: - GET: Retrieve information. - POST: Submit data to be processed. - PUT: Update or replace existing data. - DELETE: Remove data.

Database

An organized collection of structured information, or data, typically stored electronically in a computer system. Examples include relational databases like PostgreSQL and NoSQL databases like MongoDB.

CRUD (Create, Read, Update, Delete)

The four basic operations for managing data in a database or persistent storage.

Authentication

The process of verifying the identity of a user or system, often through credentials like username and password.

Authorization

The process of allowing or denying users access to resources based on their identity and roles.

JSON (JavaScript Object Notation)

A lightweight data interchange format easy for humans to read and write, and easy for machines to parse and generate. JSON is a common format for APIs to exchange data.

Testing

The process of evaluating a system or its components to determine whether it satisfies specified requirements. Unit testing, integration testing, and end-to-end testing are common types of software tests.

Debugging

The process of identifying, analyzing, and removing errors or bugs found in software.

www.ingramcontent.com/pod-product-compliance
Lightning Source LLC
Chambersburg PA
CBHW071113050326
40690CB00008B/1208